MAKING IT
TO
Monday

Published in Canada, for Global Distribution by YGTMedia Co.
www.ygtmedia.co/publishing

To order additional copies of this book:
publishing@ygtmedia.co

Edited by Rachel Small and Christine Stock

Interior design and typesetting by Doris Chung

Cover design by Michelle Fairbanks

eBook by Ellie Sipilä

Author Photo by Marlee MacLean

Cover Illustration by Lyon Road Art LLC

TORONTO

MAKING IT
TO
Monday

JENNIFER NUNES

Table of Contents

This book is dedicated to the people responsible for its content.

To my supportive and incredible husband and partner, Paul. You saw and loved me while I was still learning to do that for myself. You have been my greatest support, for which I am eternally grateful. Thank you for seeing my ability to complete this even when I could not. And to our children, Lorren and Dominic. Your resilience, strength, joy, and determination have inspired me in more ways than I could ever describe. You are the loves of my life.

Introduction

The evening of January 25, 2018, was mundane. Boring, even. I put my baby and toddler to bed and began the typical nighttime routine of a tired parent. I didn't know that the next day, my whole world would explode.

This book chronicles the weeks and months that followed that fateful day. I'd never felt more emotion. I'd never felt more alone, or more exhausted. And as odd as it might sound, I'd also never felt more loved. I'd never realized the depths of my strength.

At that time, I craved the camaraderie, empathy, and guidance of others who had walked a similar path. Despite wonderful doctors and the support of online groups, I found myself wishing for something more tangible, something in-depth and personal that I could turn to for connection. A story I could cheer for and see myself in—to give myself hope for the future.

I hope this book is that for you. I'm as honest as I can be, and it gets dark. It may trigger some painful emotions. But if there's one thing I've learned from this experience and from my career as a registered social worker, it's that when you let yourself go to those dark places and feel those dark feelings, you're also able to find light that's brighter than ever before. Start by telling yourself this: "I am going to be okay, even if this isn't okay." You don't have to believe it right now. You probably don't. I didn't at first either. And it's true.

The darkness doesn't last forever, but change can—and that's a beautiful thing.

I used to have trouble relinquishing control. When someone said, "Here, let me handle that responsibility for you," I interpreted it as a personal failure. It fed a narrative that I wasn't good enough. Shifting to a new, more positive and self-compassionate mindset was critical in building strength and resilience on this journey. I had to learn to LET. THINGS. GO. I encourage you to do the same. Start talking back to that negative voice in your head. It can eat you alive otherwise.

I am who I am because of my experiences. Becoming a mother was the most exciting and challenging transition of my life. The amount I've learned in the past seven years is almost comical. My formal education pales in comparison. I've learned how unimportant 97 percent of things in life are. I've learned that living a happy, healthy life starts with self-care, compassion, and acceptance. Communication is critical. I've also learned how important it is to distance yourself from people who don't make you feel like the best version of yourself. I understand now how difficult times really do provide the best opportunity to grow and connect with those you love, including yourself.

The qualities I possess are very much in everyone. They're in you, whether you see it or not. I hope this story inspires you to recognize your strength and general awesomeness. Let's stop waiting to achieve the goal. Let's start celebrating the journey.

Let's celebrate making it to Monday.

ONE

The Day It Happened

On Thursday, January 25, 2018, I put my son, Dominic, to bed. I watched a bit of TV, washed bottles, prepped for the next day, and went to sleep. At 4:15 a.m. I woke up to the light of the monitor. Dominic was stirring in his crib. He wasn't crying but whining and moving back and forth while eating his hand and grabbing his ear. Classic signs of teething pain. When would that darn tooth break the surface?

My husband, Paul, and I were in the process of sleep training Dominic, but I usually couldn't wait longer than a few minutes before getting out of bed and going to him, especially if our eldest was sleeping. This time when I picked him up, his body seemed tense, which was unusual. I gave him a dose of ibuprofen to help with the pain and then rocked him in my arms, his head on my shoulder. Normally this would send Dominic drifting happily back to sleep.

This time was different.

He kept fidgeting and moving. He seemed agitated. I didn't nurse him overnight anymore but hoped that it would help to settle him until the ibuprofen kicked in. I assumed our position on the couch, the one we'd been in hundreds of times before, and began nursing. He latched for perhaps five minutes and then popped off and started crying—hard. It was a loud, shrill cry. Not Dominic-like. It woke my husband, our daughter, and our tenant in the basement.

I started to get nervous. I could feel my own body tense. Both our heart rates crept higher. I tried rocking and walking around with him to calm him down. "Shhh, shhh, shhh. What's wrong, honey? These silly teeth. It's going to be okay," I cooed.

Paul met us in the kitchen and offered to give it a shot. He had the magic touch with the kids when they wouldn't settle for me. He cradled Dominic and rocked him gently. Our son calmed briefly but quickly started back up again. I'd love to say that at this point I knew something was majorly wrong, but I didn't. I felt a twinge in my gut but convinced myself that his gums were really sore and this was part of normal development. My mind often went to the worst-case scenario, and I was working hard at not being so anxious.

After about forty-five minutes of off-and-on crying I said to Paul, "If he doesn't settle by 6:00 a.m., I'm taking him to the hospital. A baby shouldn't cry for more than two hours for no apparent reason." I was repeating what I'd read on some parenting-preparation website years ago. In that moment, the text box from my computer screen was glaring at me in my mind.

Dominic refused a bottle, refused my breast, and couldn't get comfortable. Around 5:35 a.m. he finally fell asleep, in Paul's arms. Paul tried to put him back in his crib, but that only agitated him, and he woke up and started crying again. I then placed him beside me in my bed and rubbed his tummy until he settled, about five minutes later. *Sweetie*, I thought, *you just need to sleep. You're exhausted!* We fell asleep together as Paul went off to work, and I believed the worst was over.

Around 6:30 a.m. he stirred and made noise but didn't cry. I gently patted his stomach, and he went back to sleep. He looked so peaceful and little in our big bed.

At 7:00 a.m. I assumed the normal morning routine. I got our daughter, Lorren, out of bed, brushed our teeth, and started the day while letting Dominic sleep in my bed, with pillows on the edge to ensure he didn't roll off. I knew how tired he'd be from all that crying and discomfort and figured he'd sleep later into the morning than usual. I returned to my room every twenty minutes or so to check on him, and my nerves were eased every time I saw his chest and tummy rise and fall in his natural breathing rhythm.

But at 8:15 a.m. I felt that twinge in my gut getting worse. He'd been sleeping far longer than usual. This time when I went to check on him, I opened the door fully, forgetting that there was a bag hanging on the inside door handle. The bag fell to the floor with a *THUD*. Normally this would have scared him awake and caused him to cry. He moved around as if he were waking up but nothing more. Reassured that he was moving, I figured he was likely waking up from a deep sleep. A few minutes later I returned—he was fast asleep again.

My anxiety level started to rise, so I checked his breathing. His stomach rose and fell. His forehead wasn't warm. All seemed normal. I returned to my daughter in the living room. To this day, I struggle with an indescribable amount of guilt and shame for deciding in that moment to let him continue sleeping. I even took a photo of him because he looked so sweet. It makes me sick to think of that photo.

About twenty minutes later, at almost 9:00 a.m., I was sitting on the couch while my daughter watched an episode of *Peppa Pig*. *This is ridiculous*, I thought. *He's slept long enough to catch up on the missed sleep.* I decided he needed to wake up. I'm not sure if it was my intuition that something was wrong or my type A personality that loves to keep a consistent schedule that prompted this response. Maybe both.

I opened the door, walked in slowly, and called his name gently so as not to scare him awake. He didn't respond. *Thump, thump.* I could feel my heartbeat quicken as I got closer to him. He started to open his eyes, but it appeared to be a lot of work for him. I felt queasy. Something wasn't right. I stroked his face and said, "Good morning, handsome," as I always did, perhaps a bit more nervously than usual. It was then that I noticed a change in his breathing pattern—one that hadn't been there when I'd checked on him ten minutes earlier. He'd take a breath then hiccup a little before the next one. Pure fear set in and adrenaline took over.

I scooped him up in a last-ditch effort to wake him fully. On any other day, my picking him up while he was half-awake would have pissed him off so much that he'd flail his arms as if to say "Hey! I haven't had a good stretch yet!" Not this morning. He was awake but barely responsive.

I immediately called the doctor. "Don't freak out," I murmured to myself as I waited to connect.

"Just talk to the doctor, explain what's happening. He's not overly warm, he's awake, he's looking at you. Just talk to the doctor and don't freak out. Everything is okay."

The office administrator answered the phone. In my best attempt at a "I'm a concerned mother but not totally freaking out" voice, I explained what I was seeing. She said seven critically validating and important words: "Just take him to the emergency department." She was calm about it, almost casual. I told myself not to panic and frighten my daughter, who was following me around the house asking what was happening. I realize now just how receptive and smart she is and was, even at two and a half years old.

I called 911 immediately from the landline (we still had one of those at the time) and was put on hold. "You've got to be kidding me!" I said aloud, hearing the tremble in my voice. I grabbed my cell phone with shaking hands and called my mom while waiting on hold for 911 dispatch. No answer. *Maybe she's already on her way over*, I thought hopefully. We'd planned for her to visit that day. I then contacted my neighbor Vicky and explained that I was calling an ambulance for Dominic but would need someone to stay with Lorren until my mother arrived. She told me she was around the corner and would be right there.

I went into Dominic's room and my daughter followed us in, asking, "What's wrong with Dominic? Is he a little bit sick?"

"Yes, honey," I replied. "Dominic isn't feeling well, so Mommy is calling for an ambulance—that's a really cool truck with lights and a siren—to take us to see the doctor at the hospital. Don't worry, though, he's going to be okay." I'm not sure who I was trying to convince.

After a minute and a half (that felt like four hours), I was connected with Emergency Medical Services dispatch. I explained that Dominic, seven and a half months old, was lethargic, experiencing a change in his breathing pattern, and not easily rousable.

"We're on our way and two streets away."

I changed Dominic's diaper and kept saying, "It's okay, sweetie, you're going to be okay. I love you. We're going to figure this out. It's going to be okay. Hang in there, baby."

I quickly changed out of my old pajama pants but forgot to change the rest of my clothes and grab socks. I still had on my nightshirt, no bra. I hadn't showered in two, maybe three days. I finally got a hold of my mother and explained matter-of-factly what was happening—no need to freak her out more than she would have on her own (the apple doesn't fall far from the tree). She was on her way. I also called Paul to tell him that something wasn't right with Dominic and the doctor had recommended heading to the hospital. I didn't want to freak him out either, knowing that he had a half hour drive from work. I was officially in my social worker "crisis response" mode. I explained that we were going in an ambulance to the nearest emergency room: Credit Valley Hospital.

"Should I leave work, you think?" he asked me.

"Yeah, I think you should. Meet us at Credit Valley."

EMS arrived about a minute after I ended the call with my husband. I was shaking from my core but using my soft "mother voice" to speak to Dominic and Lorren, trying to shelter my daughter from what I knew was a traumatic event in the making. I lay Dominic on the couch, and at least three paramedics checked his vitals and prepared the stretcher for us.

"Have you been out of the country recently, miss?" one of the paramedics asked me.

"No, why?" I replied.

"The suitcases," he said, gesturing across the room.

I'd forgotten that I'd left them on the floor in the living room so I could slowly start to pack for our first family vacation, scheduled to take place in a week and a half.

Looking around the room, I felt as if everything were happening in slow motion. When I look back on it now, I swear I could see myself standing in the room, as if having an out-of-body experience.

What the hell is happening? He was totally fine yesterday. Why didn't I take him to the hospital early this morning? Why didn't I wake him up sooner? Is he going to be okay? What kind of mother am I?

Lorren snapped me back into real time and asked if Dominic was going to the doctor's now. "Yes, sweetie," I answered.

"Can I come too?" she asked, in her adorable toddler voice. I apologized and told her that she couldn't. In an attempt to distract her, I told her that she could play across the street at her friend's house. By then, Vicky had arrived with her son. She got Lorren into her boots and coat and did her best to bribe her with the promise of getting to play with her daughter's toys while she was at preschool. She did her best to keep Lorren distracted and calm until my mom arrived. Still, Lorren started crying. I didn't even hear it. I was in shock.

The paramedics called the hospital to tell them we were on our way. Then they gestured for me to pick up Dominic. I ripped my boot trying to pull it on with one hand while holding Dominic in the other. The paramedics offered to help, so I handed Dominic to one of them. They put him on the stretcher while I got my boots on, forgetting socks and a coat, and we headed into the ambulance. Another neighbor was standing on our driveway with wide, concerned eyes. Out of the corner of my eye I could see her mouth move—"Is everything okay?"—but I didn't have time to answer. Nor did I have an answer. I returned my gaze to Dominic, trying my very best to speak calmly to him, reassuring him he was going to be okay.

None of this felt real. I was totally numb to the Canadian January weather on my skin. My head throbbed, my chest was tight. I wasn't dizzy but couldn't see straight either.

I climbed into the ambulance behind the paramedics and Dominic. Before the doors closed, my neighbor asked me if my mom would be coming soon because Lorren was crying and asking for her. I said that she was on her way and should arrive any minute. I later learned that she got there just as the ambulance was pulling out of the driveway. Another amazing support who was there in the nick of time. I'm so grateful for this village.

Sirens on, we headed to the nearest emergency department and were ushered into a room right away. "Seven-month-old male, decrease LOC, afebrile . . ."

I recalled my days as a hospital social worker. *Decrease LOC* means "decreased level of consciousness" and *afebrile* "no fever." The team worked quickly, got an intravenous line (IV) started, and told me the pediatrician was on her way down to examine him. The fact that this all happened in a matter of minutes indicated the significance of what was going on.

My fear and anxiety levels continued to rise. I knew I could no longer stay totally calm, but I did my very best to keep my composure. The room was bright and sterile. Beeping machines and staff conversations sounded like buzzing to me. Every deep breath was shaky and unsteady.

I was standing in that room but didn't feel as though I were there.

DIAGNOSIS

The pediatrician was there within a few minutes. She ordered an IV antibiotic and CT scan with contrast then introduced herself and quickly got to business. She told me they believed the issue was one of three things.

"Given the decreased level of consciousness and the fact that he appears to be frozen on one side"—within those first ten minutes at the hospital, Dominic's right leg had bent up and appeared tight—"we think it could be either meningitis, seizures, or a stroke."

None of those options sounded good. No option was less scary than another. She then went over the risks of the CT scan with contrast, to which I responded, "Do whatever you have to do."

We headed out of the emergency department and toward diagnostics. We weren't running, but we were walking very quickly. I felt stares and heard whispers as we weaved around people in the corridor but saw nothing. My gaze stayed steadily on Dominic, who lay on a stretcher being pushed by staff. When we arrived, a room was cleared for us, no waiting whatsoever. Whatever this was, it was incredibly serious.

I picked him up, and before placing him on the bed for the CT scan,

I kissed his face and told him again that it would all be okay, that I loved him, and that I would be right outside waiting. Due to the radiation, I wasn't allowed in the room during the imaging. Then I placed him on the bed. That's when I saw it for the first time—the left side of his mouth was drooping. It hadn't been five minutes ago, when the pediatrician was speaking to me. Memories from months spent working in an adult neurology unit came flooding to my mind.

It's a stroke.

I waited right outside the door and called my mom. As calmly as possible, I explained that the doctors were investigating what it could be and that I'd let her know when I had answers. I didn't tell her about the facial droop. I didn't want to scare her. I still hoped desperately that I was wrong.

When the CT scan was finished, I followed the hospital staff transporting Dominic back to our little room in the ER. I sat beside the stretcher on his right side, stroked his hair, and softly sang the words "I love you forever," from the famous book of the same title by Robert Munsch, over and over. He seemed to respond to the sound of my voice and looked right at me, although his gaze appeared frozen. When the doctor returned, she asked to speak with me. She was compassionate but to the point.

"Dominic has had an ischemic stroke. We thought it was affecting the right side of his body because of the way he's positioned, but the stroke is actually on the right side of his brain and his left side has been impacted, which is why it's now limp." She showed me just how limp by moving his leg, which immediately flopped back onto the stretcher. "His right side is likely tightened due to discomfort or fear."

I heard the words but didn't fully process them. Still, my response was immediate. "Are we going to SickKids?"

The Hospital for Sick Children, or SickKids, is a world-renowned hospital in downtown Toronto. People come from all over the world for specialized treatment here. It's where I expected we'd be transferred.

"Yes, we've called the stroke team and they're sending someone to pick him up now."

I'd never heard of a pediatric stroke before and hadn't realized that it was common enough to require its own team. "What are the next steps?"

"We've started him on a blood thinner and discontinued the antibiotic."

Paul walked in moments later. I tried to keep the explanation brief and matter-of-fact. The doctor did the same. My husband cried as I held him. "My baby boy" is all I remember him saying. The next fifteen minutes felt like an hour. Both in shock, Paul was emotional while I felt numb. Going into full-blown crisis-management mode was the only way I knew how to react in these situations. I had no control over what was happening. The only thing I could control was how I responded and managed the incoming information. I tried to take mental notes about whom I was speaking to, what they were telling me, and so on.

Past work experience had taught me that an ischemic stroke happens when a blood clot forms in one of the arteries in the brain—in Dominic's case, the middle cerebral artery in the right hemisphere. This main artery supplies blood to the majority of the right side of the brain. Visualize a tree. It has a trunk from which large branches become smaller branches and twigs as you go higher and further outward. The brain's arteries and veins are similar. Dominic's stroke occurred just off the trunk, in a large branch. At least 50 percent of his right hemisphere had become a black hole. Doctors described the tissue as being "melted"—it was held together by the tissue around it. This melted tissue would likely scar over time and become unusable. Not much in that hemisphere would be functional again.

The brain's hemispheres have separate functions. The right hemisphere controls the left side of the body. Creativity, intuition, and the uptake of novel information is generally governed by this hemisphere. Physical movement of the left side of the body is also controlled by this area.

This stroke had caused serious damage to a large portion of our baby's brain.

How the HELL had this happened to a baby? A perfectly healthy baby. He'd had no issues: no cardiac concerns, no vascular disease, no genetic disorders that we knew of. He was tested for all the possible causes of stroke, and they all came back negative. They called it a "medical fluke."

Two to five out of 100,000 children have a stroke between twenty-eight days and eighteen years of age.[1] It's more common in utero, at a rate of about 1 in 2,500, and this is the main cause of cerebral palsy.[2] In certain cases of ischemic strokes, the cause of remains unknown.[3] Dominic fits into that category. Not knowing the cause of the stroke is still difficult to this day. It took years for me to reach acceptance about this. We may never have a medical reason for why it happened.

Learning that what had happened was rare didn't decrease my anxiety—it increased it. I'm generally a rational person who uses fact-and-evidence evaluation to manage and lower my anxiety. But as it turns out, when the worst and very unlikely scenario happens, it does a number on the psyche. If this could happen for no known reason, what was to say some

other bad and rare things wouldn't happen? It was a mind trick like no
other, and one of the major hurdles I'd need to work through to remain
positive and optimistic in the months to come.

CONTACTING PEOPLE

I called my mother first and tried to downplay the situation, stating only
facts and remaining optimistic about anything we were uncertain of—as
if I were checking items off the crisis-management "to-do list" I used as
a social worker. I reassured her by saying they had an entire stroke team
at SickKids. "This happens often enough to warrant an entire team, so
no need to panic," I said. "They'll be able to give us more information
once we're there." I must have sounded like a prerecorded voice. One
telltale sign of shock. I could tell that my mom was trying not to cry.

My dad was in Florida on holiday with his nephew at the time, and it
was decided it would be best for me to call and speak to him directly. I
have no idea if that was my idea or someone else's. My dad has a genetic
disorder that puts him at a higher risk of developing blood clots. I knew
he'd assume this gene had been passed down to Dominic and I'd need
to manage his reaction.

When he answered the phone, I suggested he sit down. He immediately got short with me. "What's going on? Don't tell me to sit down!"
My father's anxiety response is anger (fight). A trait we share.

I pressed on. "Dad, I'm trying to stay calm, and I need you to be calm
or I'll start yelling." Something in my voice must have resonated with
him because, unlike many other times, he listened to me.

"I'm sitting down," he said, a bit more calmly. "What is it?"

After I'd told him what had happened, he immediately asked if he should come home. I told him there was no point running to the airport at this moment. We didn't have any information on what was to come. I encouraged him to stay there, where it was warm, and promised to call him when I had more information. Again, monotonous, calm, and to the point. First rule of crisis management: *stay calm*.

Paul and I decided that I should be the one to call his mother. My husband seemed to think I'd be able to communicate what was happening more clearly, and we didn't want to upset or confuse anyone. Same drill. I asked her to sit down and explained in my best "social worker giving bad news to a client" voice what was happening.

She began to cry. "How does a baby have a stroke?" she said. I'd been wondering the same thing. After giving her a carbon copy of the previous conversation, I said, "He's in good hands." I hoped desperately that this was true.

Despite how exhausting making phone calls was, I was in "doer" mode. I couldn't help Dominic medically. I could, however, mobilize a crisis-response team and create some sort of strategy for how to move forward. So, I did. And I made myself the captain of that team. (Hi, my name is Jen, and I'm a control freak.) Was it the brightest idea I've ever had? Probably not. Repeating the details of this horrifying event wasn't helpful to me, but I felt as though I'd failed Dominic by not taking him in overnight. Being a failure as a mother was too much to handle as I watched my son deteriorate before my eyes, so I slipped into social worker mode instead. That was easier.

I'd learned in crisis management to always stick to facts. Do not provide information that might not be true. Do not add commentary to emotional responses. Keep statements neutral.

"Hi, I need to talk to you, can you sit down? Don't panic, we're okay, but Dominic is at the hospital. He's had a stroke. Yes, a stroke." (Everyone I spoke to replied with "A what?"). "We're being transferred to SickKids any minute. They have an entire stroke team there. We're in the best hands possible."

By the third call I had it nearly down to a script.

This was what I communicated out loud. Inside, I was thinking, *What the hell is happening? What does this mean for his future? Is he going to have permanent damage? How did this happen? Why did this happen? How did I not know something was so seriously wrong? Is he going to die?* My ability to compartmentalize pervasive thoughts in those moments was pretty decent. Turns out my many years of post-secondary training were coming in handy!

This was my child. My flesh and blood. I was working so hard to keep it "together." For what? I don't know. But I had little patience for anyone who broke down. If I wasn't crying, no one else was allowed to either. I'd spout the need to be positive and strong despite my agitation. Making a toxic assumption, I thought that if someone else was breaking down, I needed to care for them and help them feel better. I obviously didn't. No one asked me to console them. I just assumed that was expected of me. Consoling people had always been part of my job. It was as if I refused to acknowledge that this was my life.

The *I'm not good enough* mantra transformed the "stay strong" message into something different from what it was—encouragement. I was so triggered by people telling me to "stay strong." The words immediately made me defensive. I was stronger than I'd ever been in my entire life. Now I had to level up? Hearing it made me feel as if I weren't doing enough. Instead of "Stay strong," I heard, "You aren't being strong enough."

My anxiety influenced that interpretation. I know now that everyone was coming from a place of compassion. The reality is, they had no clue what to say to make me feel better, and I had no clue what I wanted to hear. If someone said, "I'm so sorry," I'd reply that it wasn't their fault (because, of course, it was *mine*). There was nothing they could say that would make me feel better. They tried their best.

The calls turned into text messages quickly. I sent text messages to dozens of close family and friends, and they all started the same way: "I cannot believe I'm writing this; however, Dominic has had a stroke. We're at SickKids . . ." I turned off all my notifications and would look at my phone only when I had the energy to do so. I left just my ringer on. The hospital would always call, not text.

As the news spread throughout my big, fat Italian family (and friend group), I focused on sharing good or optimistic information. In part, this was so I could focus on the positive and capitalize on the power of perspective. It was also a way of sheltering our family from the trauma we were experiencing. When I think back, I know I didn't open up to others about how I was feeling because I didn't feel as if anyone would understand. How could they? I didn't understand it myself.

All the hopes, dreams, and visions I had of my baby growing and developing through life were being ripped away. I had no idea what was going to happen to my child, my family, or me. I was in a sort-of dream state. In this blur, I defaulted to old coping mechanisms my parents had taught me: work hard, do your best, don't complain—it could be worse. So that's what I did. I didn't realize yet that validating my emotions was different from complaining.

During that time, every minute felt like an hour and every hour felt like a day. Paul and I sat there, at our son's bedside, stroking his hair and waiting to hear what his future held. If anything.

CRISIS MANAGEMENT

I'm no stranger to shock. I see it on clients' faces all the time. And so I knew that Paul and I were likely experiencing it.

On one of the first days after Dominic was admitted to the hospital, my aunt Josie sent me a text reminding me to take notes. She knew how important this was from her own medical experience with her son. Taking her advice, I grabbed a notebook from the hospital gift shop. One day this would all be a foggy memory that I'd need to remember. I had no control over Dominic's stroke. I did, however, have control over logistical things. I could keep tabs on what needed to be done. Focus on facts, be practical, delegate domestic responsibilities. When a crisis happened at work, my anxiety would spike and adrenaline would kick in. I'd take a deep breath, try to get grounded, and then move forward. My job was to remain neutral and calm in chaotic situations. I'd spent years working in hospitals and schools practicing this skill.

Having worked in different acute-care units, I'd participated in family care conferences. In an urgent event, available key staff and the patient's caregivers would be gathered into a private room. I'd sit next to the family, supporting them as they learned critical information and next steps. I'd never expected to be on the other side of the table in one of these meetings.

Fast-forward to 5:00 p.m. on Friday, January 26, when the team ushered Paul and me into a private room to discuss the findings of the MRI (more on this shortly) and, ultimately, the severity of Dominic's stroke. Two doctors and a nurse practitioner guided us to a room around the corner from the unit, and I was immediately filled with dread. This was not good news.

Being privy to how the healthcare system works has advantages. I knew that I could advocate for care and negotiate what was offered. I knew that I could ask questions about services if they weren't offered up front. I could use the same language as the professionals and understand some of the hundreds of acronyms—I keep up with most medical jargon. I was one of the lucky ones. I recognize that most people don't have this background. The downside is that when shit hits the fan, I smell it immediately.

Crisis-response work is emotionally taxing. Rushing to a patient's bedside and trying to be a calm and comforting voice for a loved one is difficult and highly draining. After a crisis, there's typically a debrief. This is where staff support each other. Discussions happen around what took place, how staff are coping with the event, and what could be done differently in the future. It's an important part of the work to help employees avoid burnout and compassion fatigue—this is without the emotional involvement that comes with a personal relationship thrown into the mix. When it's your own life, the hurt is deeper, sharper, and sometimes harder to articulate because so many emotions and thoughts are racing through the body and mind. There's no going home at the end of the day when it's your life.

While my training was helpful to me regarding logistics, advocacy, and planning, it was harder for me to manage the emotional piece. I responded as if I were at work, but I wasn't. This was my life. My child. I went into helper mode, distracting myself from the debilitating fear, shock, and sadness just beneath the surface. There would be no debriefing the next day or a week later. I wouldn't get to go home. This was home. This reality hit months later and caused deep despair.

Being the helper meant I didn't give myself permission to grieve in those early days. I had a few moments of tears, but nothing substantial. It felt as if there were a weight sitting on my chest one-hundred-percent of the time. I didn't have time to break down, though. After all, if I allowed the floodgates to open, they might never close. I had a job to do. If I broke down, I might never be able to pick up and carry on.

I wasn't aware of my resilience and inner strength. I didn't give myself permission to feel because it wasn't safe to do so. I had too much to do. Or so I thought.

SICKKIDS HOSPITAL

Before the ambulance picked us up for the transfer that first day, I instructed Paul to go home and get some clothing and baby items (breast pump, etc.) for Dominic and me and then meet us at SickKids. Next, I called my mom, who agreed to stay at our place with Lorren, and told her to call my brother and ask him to leave work and drive Paul to the hospital. I didn't think it was safe for him to drive himself. He tried to argue that he'd be fine, but thankfully both the doctor and nurse in the ER backed me up, so he reluctantly agreed. I was checking off the to-do list.

When the stroke team from SickKids arrived, I heard the nurse from SickKids say to staff at Credit Valley that they'd seen the CT scan and had been instructed to do a "scoop and run" with Dominic. This meant there was no time to lose. Someone on the team asked, "Where's Mom?" and the nurse pointed to where I was sitting, quietly singing to Dominic. Their voices quickly lowered.

Within five minutes we were back in an ambulance, sirens on, headed to Toronto, about thirty minutes east of our home city. I kept my eyes on Dominic and fluctuated between shock, fear, and disbelief. A few times I spoke aloud to myself: "I can't believe this is happening. My beautiful little boy." I had to stay in my seat for safety purposes, but all I wanted to do was sit on the floor next to him and cuddle and sing to him.

The team was on the phone with people at the hospital figuring out logistics. Would we go through the emergency department or straight to the Pediatric Intensive Care Unit (PICU)? Could they start an IV before he arrived? The answer to this was no—the highway was full of potholes, and he had tiny veins. They tried a few times at red lights anyway, and it was like torture watching them. I listened to their conversations. I heard the sounds of the traffic, the equipment bouncing around on every little bump we hit. Where was I? I felt nauseous and tight. I could feel the adrenaline coursing through my body, so sitting still took more effort than usual.

We ended up going straight to the PICU, where I met what seemed like fifty doctors, nurse practitioners, nurses, medical students, etc. Dominic would need an MRI to determine the severity of the stroke. They went over the risks and benefits. "Do whatever you have to do," I said.

"He needs another IV for medications."

"Do whatever you have to do."

"He'll need a continual EEG with probes when we get back, to monitor possible seizure activity due to the trauma his brain is experiencing."

"Do whatever you have to do." I felt as if I were on repeat those first few hours.

Paul arrived with my brother, who waited in the main lobby for us—he must have been down there for several hours—and Paul and I went to the MRI waiting area together. The staff put Dominic under anesthesia so he wouldn't move, and he came out of the scan intubated because his breathing had become labored, something they'd said could happen during the scan due to the anesthetic. He was no longer breathing on his own. This was when my mind went to its darkest corner. What if he didn't leave the PICU? What if this was the beginning of the end for him?

About an hour after the MRI, a PICU physician, a stroke fellow, and a nurse practitioner asked to speak to us in a small meeting room just outside the unit. As mentioned, it was the kind of meeting I used to facilitate back in my hospital social worker days. I walked in with an awful pit in my stomach.

"Dominic has had a major ischemic stroke of the right middle cerebral artery," the physician explained. "It's from a large blood clot that completely stopped blood flow to that area of the brain. The next seventy-two hours are critical because we don't know how his brain will respond to this traumatic event. We can expect it to get worse before it gets better. His brain has experienced a large trauma. It's starting to swell, and we'll monitor how much so very closely. If the swelling continues past a certain point, surgical intervention may be required to relieve the pressure on the brain. He could have seizures from this trauma, and we'll put him on antiseizure medications if he does. We'll do a continuous electroencephalogram [EEG] on him to monitor seizure activity. Neurosurgery will follow you over the weekend. Right now, it's hour to hour for Dominic. We don't know what his brain is going to do or how it's going to react, but we are doing everything we can to minimize the effects of this stroke."

The information seemed to come all at once, like a tsunami of words. I did my best to capture the information pounding over us. The phrases *minimize the effects* and *hour to hour* stuck out in my mind. What kinds of effects? Would he have physical deficits forever? Would his cognitive development be affected? I realized it was too early for these questions. Right now, it was about survival. Making it past the seventy-two-hour mark. Making it to Monday. No one knew what would happen. No one would even talk to us about Tuesday.

I took a deep breath. Paul was crying softly beside me. I had to voice the terrifying thought yelling in my head. I didn't realize until later how professional and detached I sounded when I spoke, slow and direct.

"I don't think my husband or I realized the magnitude of the situation until now, and perhaps I still don't fully appreciate the significance of what has happened to our son. We're in shock. A lot of what you're saying is overwhelming and elusive. Are we talking about—" I cut myself off and changed my sentence. I needed to be blunter than my usual sugarcoated self. "Should I be end-of-life planning for my son?"

I didn't want to use the words, but all I could think was *What if he dies?*

"I wish I had the answer to that," the doctor replied. "We cannot say for sure because we don't know how his body will respond. We want to say no, of course, but we just don't know. Look, if this were to have happened to you or me, we'd be toast. But he's very young, and that's a good thing regarding his chances of recovery. Neuroplasticity can be astonishing, and his age is a protective factor in this case."

We'd be toast. I will never forget those words. This wasn't just a stroke; this was a really bad stroke.

Then Paul spoke. "So we just have to wait until Monday."

"Yes," the doctor responded.

Monday seemed like a million years away. The doctors, nurses, and nurse practitioners were all kind and compassionate, but the information didn't change. Dominic had to make it to Monday before anyone would talk about Tuesday. Paul and I cried, he more than I, and the meeting ended. How would we make it through the weekend? What were we going to do? What about Lorren? My mind raced as I tried to piece together a plan for next steps—an automatic response, having worked in these situations.

When I worked with clients experiencing trauma, my heart ached for them. I felt so fortunate that I could, at least, be a constant source of strength and provide them with information and resources to help them make decisions. I could offer comfort where possible and attempt to inspire strength in scary, uncertain times. At the very least, I could allow them a safe space to voice their dark thoughts and feelings—to externalize them. I didn't show a lot of emotion. I was trained to remain empathetic but neutral. Then I'd go home to my life.

Now this WAS my life, and I had nowhere to go.

I didn't want to burden Paul with the worst-case scenario playing in my mind. For all I knew he was thinking the same thing. I just stayed quiet, and the scenario kept replaying. Vividly. Right now, I had to manage. I needed to take charge, be a source of strength for my husband and our family and myself.

The most critical piece of advice I got that day was from the nurse who walked us back to the PICU after the MRI. He was encouraging us to eat something, get some sleep, etc. I found this a bit silly, thinking, *We just got here a few hours ago. How could anyone possibly think about eating or sleeping right now?*

I turned to him and said, "Please, level with me. What are we starting here—a sprint or a marathon?"

He looked at me seriously and said, "Marathon, one-hundred-percent."

WHAT-IFS

As much as I tried to stay positive and mindful, *What if he dies?* kept creeping into my head. My brain spiraled. I started to pick out the photo for his prayer card/tombstone. I thought about arrangements that would need to be made. What funeral home? How would we support our daughter through grief that she was too young to understand? How would we ever heal as a family? My brain conjured up vivid images of what that reality could look like. Would we leave his crib and furniture in his bedroom? Would it be too hard to remain in our home?

Of course, none of this was hopeful or positive, but that's where my mind went. The images were detailed. If I close my eyes, I can easily recall them, even years later. It felt as if I were looking at my life from outside my body. I could see myself within those scenarios I created in my mind. It felt like the emotional equivalent of pushing on a bruise—it already hurt, and this made it hurt more but also felt somewhat satisfying. As if the anxiety of the unknown was so unbearable that having a plan, even if it was for the worst imaginable outcome, was a morbid comfort. It gave me a sense of control, which temporarily eased my anxiety.

I couldn't talk about the what-ifs with Paul for two reasons: I didn't want to put any images in his head, in case they weren't already there, and I didn't want to make them real. Saying them out loud would have felt like evidence that my thoughts could become reality.

There's a term for this: *catastrophizing*. Catastrophizing involves fixating on the worst-case scenario to the point where it feels as though it's the most plausible outcome. Anxiety's best friend. I did this after my first child was born. It's sometimes a self-preservation tactic. Imagine the worst and prepare for it, so that when it doesn't happen, you feel relief. If I could go back, I'd tell myself to accept these images but ALSO to conjure up the opposite. *What is the best-case scenario? Think of that and daydream about the positive possibilities as well.*

The fact was that my catastrophic thinking wasn't that far from reality at that time. The worst was on the table. Even the doctor didn't know if Dominic would survive. Would he? Would I?

Not long after that horrific meeting, I spoke to a family member who encouraged me to consider visualizing healing, positivity, white light, etc. She reminded me of the importance of protecting our energy and filling Dominic's brain, heart, and soul with love and positive messages.

It couldn't hurt, I thought. So I did it. A lot. A form of meditation, it was calming for me and helped me stay positive when I was with Dominic. I like to think it helped him too. It also turned out to be an excellent lesson on just how much power perspective has to create positive neuropathways. At the end of the day, we don't always have control of the path that we're on, but we can control how we respond to the path. We can use our energy in a way that benefits us.

TWO

Waiting for Monday

Dominic had to lie flat for at least forty-eight hours poststroke. It was hospital protocol. He had three IVs, twenty probes on his head, an arterial line in his arm, an esophageal thermal probe (up the nose), and was intubated (he had a breathing tube in his mouth that went down his throat). Our cheery baby was unrecognizable. He was getting swollen from the IV fluids and lying flat, and I couldn't help but notice how small Dominic was compared to the hospital-sized crib, monitors, screens, and other medical apparatus that surrounded and engulfed his body.

Paul sat in a chair beside Dominic's crib, his head in his hands, staring at our son. He looked stunned. I stood beside him, leaning on the bed rail. We had little to no privacy from the three other beds in the room, but a few hours later, Paul broke down and repeated, "I just want my smiley baby back."

I held my husband as tightly as I could. "Look, we're going to be okay, even if this is not okay. No matter what happens, we will get through this. We must be strong for him. We have to be positive. Dominic needs positive, healing, calm energy around him. He needs us." I have no idea where I got the conviction, but I meant every single word.

Part of me didn't believe this was real life. Another part of me was planning my son's funeral. But the moment I saw my calm, strong husband breaking down, I realized that it was my turn to be that pillar of strength and stability that he so often is for me. As foreign and scary as this situation was, the surroundings were familiar to me. I could do this, at least for a little while.

I recognized shock and trauma when I saw them, and my husband had textbook symptoms. I was in shock too. Maybe it was divine intervention, maybe it was mama-bear strength, but somehow, I regained my composure and started to think clearly. I kept a journal of what symptoms Dominic was showing and what the professionals were saying because I truly didn't know if I'd remember any of this. I also wrote about how I felt and what I was eating—even if I couldn't stomach a proper meal, I would at least have a fruit and vegetable smoothie to ensure I was getting some nutrients in my body. I couldn't afford to get sick.

Paul and I determined rather quickly that we didn't want any visitors until we knew with more certainty that recovery was likely. Knowing that our parents would want to visit, we decided that first night to say that only parents/guardians were allowed in the PICU. We didn't like lying but felt it was necessary. It was already so hard to manage our emotions and process what was happening—we couldn't bear to manage the emotions of others, too. Plus, being a spiritual person who believes that energy has an impact on people's functioning, I didn't want any more sad, fearful energy around Dominic. He needed calm, healing, and positivity. No matter how hard it was, even if it took every ounce of my own energy, that was what I was going to give him.

"I cannot leave him," I said to Paul. "I cannot leave the hospital."

He graciously responded, "I know," and we decided that it would be best for Lorren if Paul went home to tuck her into bed and to try to get some sleep himself before returning to the hospital in the morning. We wanted to keep some sense of normalcy in Lorren's life during this chaotic time. I felt awful that I hadn't spoken to her since leaving in the ambulance that morning. My mother had assured me that although Lorren was upset when she first arrived on the scene, she'd bounced back quickly and was playing and talking as usual. My mother agreed to sleep at our house so that Paul could return to the hospital as soon as he woke up.

THE FIRST NIGHT

That first night was a total blur. I sat at Dominic's bedside and stroked his forehead and held his fingers. His hands and arms had too many medical instruments in them to touch, and I wasn't permitted to hold him due to "poststroke protocol." It felt awful not being able to hold my baby.

The nurse that night was a woman named Julia. An angel, she chatted with me and was friendly, compassionate, understanding, and encouraging.

She saw that I was a mom of two young children who clearly hadn't showered in a while and encouraged me to make use of the Ronald McDonald Family Room, a space on the fourth floor where parents could have a shower, a snack, or reserve a recliner for a rest.

In the PICU, patients have 24/7 nursing care at a 1:1 ratio. There's always a nurse in the room. And so, around midnight, I decided to try a shower and a nap, as I wanted to be alert the next time I spoke with a member of Dominic's medical team. I confirmed that Julia had my phone number and had her attach it to the computer screen beside Dominic's bed, in case she needed to call me. I then headed up two floors, which felt like fifty miles away.

A volunteer greeted me quietly at the door and asked me to sign in. I'd been given a badge in the PICU that indicated what unit my child was on and that I was a parent. Looking around the room, I saw several people talking quietly. Some were eating or settling in for the night on pullout couches. Each had their own child inside this building. Each was on their own medical journey. I was so grateful for that room. Not only was I able to have a shower, but I also secured a recliner in a quiet cubicle.

I slept for almost two hours, woke up in a panic, and ran back down to Dominic, who was sleeping peacefully, Julia by his side. She assured me that he hadn't woken up since I left. She and I talked some more, and then she once again gently encouraged me to attempt to get a bit more sleep. It was about 3:30 a.m. at this point. I wanted to stay with him 24/7, but there was only one place to sit in the room, and it was hard. And I knew I needed to sleep. Reluctantly, I went back to the family room and slept for another hour.

When I returned to his bedside, I just watched him for a few hours. I learned the rhythm of the breathing monitor, watching the squiggly lines go up and down in sync with his breath, and asked Julia questions about what the different lines meant; I also listened to his heart monitor, watched his blood pressure for any changes, and studied his body temperature. Beside his crib, unopened, was a brochure on pediatric strokes. *Not now*, I thought. I wasn't ready to start researching.

Looking beyond Dominic's crib, I noticed that the baby in the crib next to his was also intubated. He had a mobile that projected a cartoon field with a rainbow and playing children onto the ceiling. It played a beautiful, soft melody. Through the beeps of the monitors and the humming of machinery I could hear that sweet, soft lullaby.

I'm in a room full of children and parents going through trauma, I thought. *All different, yet so much the same.* It was an eye-opening and humbling experience. I was in awe of the nursing and support staff of this unit.

SATURDAY

Paul rejoined us Saturday morning, and we sat and watched Dominic all day. The doctors came and went, telling us when the EEG noted subclinical seizure activity. This meant that although he wasn't convulsing—which happens during the classic tonic-clonic (previously called grand mal) seizure—there was seizure activity going on in his brain. Each time they told us about seizure activity, they loaded Dominic with an additional dose of the antiseizure medication, which kept him sleepy. He hadn't woken up much at all since the stroke.

I don't remember if Paul and I spoke much that day, or what about, if we did. Certainly, it was in simple sentences, expressing fears and giving each other pep talks. Each hour that went by without bad news was a little victory.

Midday, the team decided they'd do another MRI to track the swelling and the blood clot, and in the late afternoon, they took Dominic down to the MRI room. One of my best friends, Nikita, and her husband, Jarrel, came to the hospital with food for Paul and me—a very kind gesture of love and support. We noticed them arrive in the waiting room as we watched the team take Dominic down the elevator to the MRI room (we weren't allowed in for the procedure). I hated being separated from him but was thankful for the distraction of good friends.

As soon as we were in the waiting room with them, tears welled in all our eyes. They too had a young child, about six months older than Dominic. I swallowed hard to stop myself from crying, but Paul didn't have such luck. Neither did Nikita. I tried to lighten the mood by teasing Paul, saying, "Not you too!" but immediately regretted that. Why was I trying to get him to bury his emotions just because I was burying mine? This was the most emotion he'd shown throughout our entire marriage. I knew I should be embracing it.

I finished chastising myself silently, and the four of us sat down to talk. I delivered the updates directly and matter-of-factly, but my tone was flatter than usual. Our friends were supportive but also in shock. It was difficult to believe a perfectly healthy baby could become so sick so quickly.

About thirty minutes later we left our friends and returned to Dominic's bedside to wait for his return. On his arrival, the neurosurgeon told us that the swelling in Dominic's brain had increased, and although this was to be expected in the first forty-eight to seventy-two hours, they'd have to monitor him even more closely going forward. If the swelling got worse, they'd need to operate. "It's very unlikely that I'll have to operate on Dominic, but I wanted to keep you both informed."

"Well," I replied, somewhat curtly, "with all due respect, I thought my perfectly healthy seven-month-old having a massive stroke was pretty unlikely too, so I don't know if I believe in unlikely events anymore."

I immediately apologized for my tone, and the doctor chuckled softly and nodded. He was kind and seemed to understand my response. *They must get this all the time,* I thought. *His entire career is based on anomalies and worst-case, rare scenarios.*

When the doctor left, Paul broke down again. I reminded him that the doctors had said this could happen. "It will get worse before it gets better," I said. "This is just the part that's a little worse. He's having seizures and his brain is swelling. He's still okay. Remember, they're doing another MRI late tonight to monitor the swelling so they can respond accordingly. We just have to wait and see. He can do this, and so can we." I was starting to believe it.

Meanwhile, calls and texts from friends and family kept coming in. The outpouring of love, support, positive thoughts, and prayers was overwhelming, and we were so grateful for it. A cousin encouraged me to talk positively to Dominic, even if we were unsure whether he could hear us. She reminded me that as humans, we can feel people's presence and energy, so it was important to make mine positive, loving, and healing for him. She reaffirmed that I was doing the right things, such as singing lullabies and cooing to him that he was going to be okay.

I'm his mom, I thought. *I can't help him get better right now in a medical way, but I CAN shower him with love and positive, healing talk and touch.* Focusing on this idea made me feel stronger. I hoped this would be passed on to Dominic.

Paul and I sat near his bed, and I started softly singing in our son's ear, telling him that he was "so strong, so brave, and doing so well." I visualized warm, white healing light around him and pictured him being engulfed in my loving embrace since I couldn't physically hold him. I stroked his arm and the small piece of forehead that wasn't covered in tape from the tubes or probes from the EEG.

The waiting was torture. I had so many questions, so many fears, the biggest one being *Will he make it to Monday?* I was in every parent's worst nightmare, and I took a few moments to allow my mind to go to the depths of the darkness. Then I chose to return to the present. I chose to be strong for this baby. I chose to be positive and supportive. I forced myself not to give the darkness any more of my energy than I felt absolutely necessary.

Paul encouraged me to take a nap. It took some convincing, but I returned to that quiet room on the fourth floor and reserved a recliner. There were three other individuals there, and in the silence, it felt as if we had a comfortable understanding of each other. It was the oddest sense of camaraderie I've ever experienced.

On Saturday night, the team felt that Dominic was trying to breathe on his own and were willing to attempt taking out the breathing tube.

Paul and I stood at the bedside with a respiratory therapist, a doctor, and several nurses while they removed the tube and monitored Dominic's ability to breathe. He cried a hoarse, weak cry for the first time since this journey began. It was the first time I really cried too. The doctor started to console me, telling me Dominic's crying was a positive sign, but I stopped her, saying, "These are happy tears. I can hear his voice."

I'd never been so happy to hear my son cry. He was breathing. I felt safe enough to release a bit of what I'd been holding in. After a minute I composed myself and went right back to the positive talk and visualization.

That same night, two resident physicians said that because Dominic was now on a high dose of blood thinners, they needed to monitor his blood to ensure it wasn't too thick or thin. They requested permission to put in an arterial line (a direct catheter into an artery—it looked like an IV with three caps on top and was almost the length of Dominic's entire forearm), so they wouldn't have to attempt to draw blood every twelve to twenty-four hours. It would take one tricky poke to insert, but no more pokes would be necessary when they needed blood after that point. Paul and I agreed, and they told us we could stay at the bedside while they inserted the line.

They used an ultrasound machine (or something similar) to see inside his tiny arm and locate the artery for insertion. This wasn't an easy task. Dominic, although weak and in and out of sleep, didn't like being restrained and voiced his dissatisfaction with the residents' inaccuracy in finding the artery. The residents worked for what felt like an hour, and I cringed the entire time. On several occasions, I wanted to tell them to stop altogether. Finally, the lead physician of the PICU entered the room and did just that. Dominic had to go for another MRI—they'd have to try again later. My heart hurt for him, knowing he'd be put through this again. Thankfully, on the second try they were able to insert it much faster (on the opposite arm), and once it was inserted Dominic calmed and fell asleep.

The third MRI happened around 10:00 p.m. that night, after Paul had gone home to put Lorren to sleep. I knew he was staying up to hear the results of this test. I also refused to go to bed, although the nurse said it might be an hour before the test was done. I waited at the bedside anyway and closed my eyes. Over an hour later, the on-call doctor arrived to let me know what they'd found: the swelling in the brain had remained consistent, and they were pleased with that. They would continue to monitor him via EEG and do neurological checks hourly and reassess in the morning. That was good news to me! Any sign of stability was the equivalent of improvement in my mind. We'd made it another few hours without needing surgery.

I told Paul the news and hoped that this information would give him the peace he needed to sleep. I couldn't imagine how hard it must have been to leave one child, nearly unconscious and hooked up to tubes, at the hospital and return home to another who was completely healthy and full of questions and energy, with no understanding of what was happening. He gives me kudos for being strong during this time, but I don't think he realizes the kind of strength it takes to be able to do what he did.

Before the day ended, I received word that my dad had booked a flight home from Florida. He was aware he couldn't visit the PICU but wanted to be close to home and support us however he could. I'm truly grateful for this. He was there to help my mom and give Lorren a sense of normalcy, since he used to babysit her daily when I was working.

SUNDAY

On Sunday afternoon, my parents brought Lorren to the hospital to see me—I hadn't spoken to her since Friday. While I couldn't wait to see her, I was nervous about how to answer any questions she might have. She seemed bigger and more mature than she'd been two days ago. Her sentences were longer and more complex and she was more affectionate than usual. I embraced the cuddles and hugs and told her how much I loved her, always and forever, no matter what. She asked if Dominic was still feeling sick, and I said that he was but that the doctors and nurses were taking good care of him. She trusted this response and quickly began talking about the amazing glass elevators in the hospital.

After an hour of playing with her in the atrium, I began to get anxious—I'd been away from the bedside for so long. What if Dominic woke up and I wasn't there? We said our goodbyes, and Lorren returned home with my parents.

It was heartbreaking seeing her leave without us.

During the first thirty-six hours poststroke, Dominic continued to have subclinical seizures. His body temperature crept up with each hour that passed, and Tylenol wouldn't break the fever. In an attempt to regulate his temperature, hospital staff lay him flat on a cooling mat and monitored the temperature probes carefully. Dominic had nothing but a diaper and tubes to cover his body. At times his little legs would shiver, so I asked his nurse if he could have a thin cotton blanket to cover his legs and provide some comfort. Thankfully, the nurse, Kim, found a little blanket and brought it to him.

It's hard to describe what it felt like seeing my baby like this; I wouldn't wish it on my worst enemy. He didn't look like himself, and he wasn't responsive except to painful stimuli or to the sound of my voice or Paul's (if awake, which was rare). Still, I tried to stay as positive and strong as I could. We were almost at Monday. One hour at a time. One hour closer to reaching that pivotal threshold.

As the weekend dragged on at what felt like a snail's pace, Paul and I noticed that Dominic's body was getting puffier. Every once in a while he'd try to open his eyes, but it became more and more difficult for him to do that. By Sunday afternoon, his eyes were little round balls. He seemed to be swelling by the hour. I'd informed the nurse about our concerns on more than one occasion, and she said it was likely due to lack of movement, his lying flat, and the IV fluids (he couldn't consume anything orally).

"Is there something you can do to alleviate the swelling?" I asked. It couldn't be comfortable, and I wanted him to be able to open his eyes and see us if he had the strength and ability to do so.

That evening, the doctor agreed to start him on a diuretic to reduce the buildup of excess fluid in his body. She also said that if all went well that night, I'd be able to hold him tomorrow. The excitement of that possibility carried me through the rest of the night. I slept about four hours, in two separate blocks. This routine was already starting to feel normal.

As Paul was getting ready to leave for the night, I told him to prepare himself for the next day.

"Why?"

"Tomorrow is Monday, so the 'full' team will be in tomorrow doing daily rounds." This meant more people to meet and possibly more information to take in. As well, all the outpatient clinics would be open, so parking would be trickier. Plus, it was MONDAY. The day we'd been waiting for. If we could get to dinnertime on Monday, we'd be past the critical seventy-two-hour period. I was starting to feel hopeful. Dominic hadn't shown any seizure activity since Saturday night. The medication was starting to work. If we could make it to Monday, we could make it through anything.

MONDAY

Monday morning, I was at the bedside by 5:20 a.m., a coffee in hand. My sister-in-law had dropped off Starbucks gift cards within twenty-four hours of our arriving at the hospital—a truly appreciated gesture. At this point, I was running on Starbucks coffee and a smoothie a day. I was also pumping four times a day in an attempt to keep my abysmal breastmilk supply going. I didn't know if Dominic would be able to nurse again but wanted him to at least have the option. The nurses would take whatever milk I pumped and freeze it.

Dominic looked a lot less swollen, especially in his beautiful face, which was starting to take its original shape again. He'd opened his eyes for Paul the night before for the first time, and he'd done the same for me several times throughout the night, which gave me added strength and much-needed energy. I kept reminding myself that today was the day I'd get to hold him, and I was so excited for that moment to come.

As the doctors started their rounds, around 7:00 a.m., I was ready, notebook in hand. I was informed that he'd had another subclinical seizure overnight and had therefore been loaded with an additional dosage of the antiseizure medication, which explained his drowsiness that morning. I was told that after twelve to twenty-four hours of no seizure activity in the ICU, the EEG probes would be removed. He was still getting his maintenance dose of phenobarbital, an anti-epileptic medication, twice per day—and this would likely be his new reality for at least a year, possibly longer. After the brain experiences a trauma, the likelihood of having seizures goes up significantly, especially in children.

"Since he's already had more than two seizures, he's at higher risk, so we'll send him home on antiseizure medications," the neurosurgeon explained.

This was the first time I'd heard a staff member talk about the future. It wasn't ideal, but man did it feel amazing to hear someone talk about Dominic going home, even if it was going to look different.

No surgical intervention had been required to this point, and the staff felt as though he was stabilizing, other than the seizure activity. The neurosurgeon said he looked "wonderful" so far and that the likelihood of needing surgery went down by the day. The diuretics were working to reduce the swelling in his body, and he'd been started on continuous low-volume feeds through a nasal gastric (NG) tube to ensure he was getting nutrients. An NG tube is inserted through the nose, down the throat, and directly into the stomach. It allows a person to consume liquid without the need to swallow. In addition to the breastmilk I'd been pumping, I'd also provided the hospital with formula, to try to keep Dominic's food as consistent as possible. The doctor then confirmed that since initial stroke protocol had been followed, Dominic could now tilt up to 30 degrees.

The neurosurgeon explained to me again that the stroke was in the middle cerebral artery, in one of the main "branches"—the area of the brain mainly responsible for motor and sensory function. This could possibly affect his left arm and leg and the left side of his face. "We feel confident he'll walk and talk one day," the neurosurgeon said, "but he'll likely have noticeable weakness forever, particularly in his arm and hand. The stroke damaged brain tissue in multiple areas of the right hemisphere, including the temporal lobe and basal ganglia and a part of the frontal lobe."

There was no way to know exactly what it would look like as he grew, and this, the doctors said, was a good thing. His brain was still developing, and although a large chunk of it had died in the stroke, new "real estate" in the brain could take over certain functions normally controlled by the affected right side. They recommended genetic testing for future planning. Paul and I agreed, and I offered information regarding my and my father's genetic mutations to assist in the search for what had caused such a large stroke in such a seemingly healthy boy.

Finally, after I'd asked all my other questions, I asked in a small voice if

I'd get to hold my son that day. The doctor in charge of the ICU looked at me, smiled, and said, "I think that sounds like a great plan."

THE FIRST EMBRACE

I'll never forget the moment Dominic was born. Two nurses and my husband stood beside the doctor, who made a funny joke. We all started laughing. I remember saying, "He's going to come out!" through my heaps of laughter. The doctor was kind and calm and a few seconds later I pushed for the final time (of three—I know, it was magical; I wish this kind of labor on every woman). Then he was on my chest, taking his first breaths.

I looked at his squishy red face and thought, "What a way to enter the world, to the sounds of laughter." His current positive demeanor makes me wonder if this had an impact on him.

He lay on my chest doing skin-to-skin for over an hour and seemed ready to take the world by storm after his first feeding. Paul and I guessed his weight, and both of us guessed too low. He had a dimple in his chin, and his cheeks and nose were round. I felt calm and serene in his presence. He was perfect, just as so many children are to their mothers when they finally get to meet them. It makes the months of being kicked around from the inside worth it.

On January 29, 2018, I had that same excited but calm feeling. The scare of potentially losing my child and the million questions that Paul and I still had about his future—it all melted away at the thought of holding him.

When I got the green light that Monday morning, I assumed my position in the vinyl chair at his bedside. It was painfully uncomfortable. My backside had taken a beating that weekend—I'd been sleeping in chairs, hunching over pumping, and sitting or standing at Dominic's bedside for hours. Hoping to get some skin-to-skin time, I took off my sweater so I wore nothing but an undershirt. I needed help getting him in my arms due to the hemiplegia (weakness on one side) and the plethora of devices and tubes attached to him. When the nurse lay him in my arms, I adjusted the tubes and made sure to be gentle with his arterial line. His body was warm, but it felt different; foreign even. It had very little muscle tone or tension, and the left side was totally limp. But the joy of being able to hold him again outweighed any concerns I had about this.

I could see that he was trying to move his right arm, but the arm board protecting the arterial line and the IV constricted it. The EEG probe wires had been carefully placed over my arm, so I didn't tug at them. I had to delicately place his left arm near my chest to offer support but also not bother the IVs. Once we got ourselves situated, he fell asleep quickly in my arms. It was as close to euphoric as I've ever been. I realized how much I'd taken for granted in my life up to this point. The simple pleasure of holding my baby was more than enough to make me smile from deep within my soul for the first time in a long time.

I stared at Dominic, kissed his forehead, and gently moved my thumb along his hand. I spoke to him softly, sang "I love you forever," and commended his bravery and strength, feeling totally at peace. I did more visualizations with the idea of cocooning us both in healing energy. While he and I shared this wonderful moment, however, Dominic's heart rate began to drop. Since the stroke, it hadn't gone below 110 beats per minute (bpm). When doctors were poking and prodding the rate would go up—during the arterial-line insertion, it had reached 180 bpm. It had become clear to Paul and me that the beats per minute coincided with how agitated he was. Now, the rate was dropping, from 105 to 103 to 101 to 95 to 93. I started to get nervous.

Kim was present the entire time and kept her eye on the heart monitor as well. Keeping her cool, she repositioned Dominic slightly, but he didn't respond. I could feel my own heart rate rise, and the fear I'd felt Friday morning started to return. Suddenly he started to move his unaffected side and showed some agitation. A wave of relief washed over me. I could see Kim relax as well, and when I voiced my fear, she admitted that she too had been a bit nervous.

"He's feeling so happy and safe in your arms," she said. "He's in the deepest sleep he's been in since he arrived." I took that as a massive compliment. Two hours of holding Dominic went by in what felt like five minutes. Then it was Paul's turn to hold his little boy. Watching my two boys together was another joyous moment—one I hadn't known I'd enjoy so much. I decided to take these few hours for what they were: a victory and a blessing. They were what I'd needed to strengthen and reenergize.

Throughout our time in the hospital, Dominic had been emitting what nurses called a "neurological" cry (a result of the brain trauma and healing process). It was a dull, low-pitched sound mixed with a whine, and he'd make it in his sleep. Sometimes it was apparent that he was uncomfortable, but other times we couldn't figure out what was causing it. It always sounded eerie to me because it wasn't his normal "I'm frustrated" or "I'm hungry" or "I'm tired" cry. I'm an expressive person, so it worried me to think that his ways of communicating could be affected by the stroke—that was just one of many scary thoughts that floated into my mind. But since I'd decided to focus on the positive, after experiencing that thought I moved on to something else. It didn't feel like the time to process the what-ifs. Right now was a time for strength and healing. I would process later.

Paul had brought Dominic's sound machine with him to the hospital that day. We hoped that the familiar sounds from his bedroom at nighttime would be a comfort and would help him distinguish between night and day. One of the nurses had told me it was common for babies to get confused about what time of day it was in the ICU, since they often slept throughout the day and didn't go outside. This could lead to baby delirium. So far, Dominic had been sleeping somewhat consistently throughout the night and most of the day. If he did wake up and fuss or let out that "neuro" cry, I (or the nurse, if I was showering or napping) would gently hold Dominic's forehead and pat his tummy. I'd sing "I love you forever" and remind him of how strong and brave he was, and that he was doing so well. Within five to ten minutes, he'd drift back to sleep.

We'd also brought two teddy-bear blankets from home (blankets that had stuffed-animal heads). Paul and I would each keep one in our shirts. Paul saw it as a friendly competition—why should Dominic smell only Mommy and not Daddy, too? The nurses said our sense of humor was important and a positive sign, even for Dominic.

That night, when Paul got ready to leave, he tucked in his blanket near Dominic's shoulder, so that it was cuddled into his neck. I did the same thing on the other side of him when I went to bed. An hour or two later, a nurse turned Dominic onto his side, and when I came back downstairs to check on him, he was holding the blankets in his hands while sleeping. He looked adorable—he'd started resembling a baby again.

We'd gotten to Monday.

THREE

Next Steps

Tuesday morning, I arrived at the bedside just before 5:00 a.m. Dominic's sound machine was quietly playing ocean waves. I held and caressed his leg, and he seemed very calm. The first day after the critical seventy-two-hour period was over. Going on several days with little sleep, I was zombie-like. The last few days had felt like an odd, vivid nightmare that had gone on and on. I didn't know what to think or feel about what had happened. I spoke to Dominic as he lay in his crib, and I wrote in my journal about how proud of him I was, about how well I thought he was doing. No surgery had been needed so far, and the seizures had been managed with medicine since Sunday night.

When the doctors arrived that morning, they finally started to talk about the future. They felt confident that Dominic would one day walk, talk, go to school, etc., but that it would take a lot of rehabilitation. No one could give us timelines regarding when these milestones would occur—there was no way to know. Each baby is unique, as is their neuro-plasticity (more on this concept shortly). All we knew for certain was that it would be a long road to recovery. The doctors felt Dominic was now starting that portion of the journey.

The change in their communication style was a major positive shift. Before this point, they hadn't even mentioned rehabilitation. The relief was huge, and weight lifted off my chest with every conversation about recovery and the future. I didn't care how long the road was. Having a road at all was something to be celebrated. I declared to Dominic at his bedside and in my journal that although it might not always be easy, Paul and I would be there for him and support him in any way we could, and that we loved him no matter what the outcome.

The doctors told us that there were two options for rehabilitation: inpatient rehab in Toronto or outpatient rehab at home. Within a few days, however, it was no longer an option—Dominic was totally paralyzed on the left side and would need inpatient rehabilitation to maximize his recovery. He had facial paralysis complete with the wide left eye and the droop around the lip. There was no movement in the hand, arm, or leg. He couldn't sit up or even be held without significant support. Holding him felt like holding a sixteen-pound newborn mixed with gelatin. As well, the muscles in his tongue were partially paralyzed, preventing him from being able to do things he was born able to do: He couldn't breastfeed or drink from a bottle. He couldn't swallow food without choking. He couldn't make the sounds that he used to (*ba-ba, da-da, ga-ga*, etc.). The simplest movements, ones we make thousands of times a day, ones we take for granted, Dominic would have to relearn from scratch.

On that Tuesday morning, he had fewer tubes coming out of him, and the EEG probes were coming off later that day. All that remained were the arterial line, the heparin (blood thinner) IV, and the NG tube. Major progress. Around 8:30 a.m., I was blown away by his alertness. His eyes were more open than they'd been since Friday, the swelling was almost completely gone, and he responded happily when I sang "The Wheels on the Bus" and "Peekaboo I Love You." He even went so far as to attempt to touch his NG tube, the first sign of frustration since the night this all started.

The nurses reminded me that a frustrated baby is an alert baby. A good sign. "It means he's aware of his surroundings." Still, I felt helpless and wished I could take all the discomfort away. I reminded Dominic (and myself) for the millionth time how well he was doing and that we would all be okay, even if this wasn't. Later that morning he began to move his right (unaffected) hand quite a lot. I wasn't sure if that was because he wanted to bend it (it was being blocked by the IV board) or because of the brain trauma. When it wasn't moving, it was holding a teddy blanket.

A follow-up MRI would be done on Wednesday, to make sure there was no bleeding in the brain, assess how the brain was reacting to the stroke, and note any changes in swelling. If it went well, the doctors would consider changing the continuous heparin to another anticoagulant, which Dominic would receive regularly. This would mean reducing the number of IVs, removing the arterial line, and hopefully moving out of the PICU to the neurology unit. I started to get excited but tried to slow myself down. One step at a time.

FIRST VISIT, FIRST NIGHT AWAY

That afternoon, my parents brought Lorren to visit Dominic for the first time since the stroke. Paul and I had decided to lift the "visitor ban" for Lorren and the grandparents. Paul's parents were recovering from colds, so they decided to wait a few more days before visiting, to be safe.

A child life specialist spoke to Paul and me about preparing Lorren to see Dominic in the hospital with IVs and the NG tube. We were concerned about my parents seeing these as well. The specialist gave us a metaphor that was integral to helping us understand how young children process and cope with situations like ours. "For you and Paul, what you're going through is like being in a river," she said. "The current may be strong at times, peaceful at others, but you don't get out of the water. For children, like Lorren, it's a puddle. They can jump in, splash around, and jump right out again." That depiction couldn't have been more accurate.

Once Lorren had arrived with my parents, we all sat together on a bench just outside the unit. Here, the child life specialist showed Lorren pictures she'd taken of Dominic and the PICU, so she would have an idea of what she was about to see (and so would my parents). When we entered Dominic's room, Lorren was so happy to see him that she didn't care about her surroundings—a blessing of the innocence and naivety of childhood. I wished we could all see the person within with such ease. My parents held it together well; at least in front of us. Lorren got a little stuffed turtle from the child life specialist that said *SickKids* on it and Dominic got a matching one, so they could always be reminded of each other. Lorren decided to name her turtle Dominic, so we named Dominic's Lorren. It was the first of many moments where Lorren would melt my heart and blow me away with her compassion and empathy. Her resilience throughout the experience was inspiring.

She played pretend, making up stories and characters, and included Dominic for a few minutes. Then she started to color by the bedside, effectively "jumping out of the puddle." Seeing her interact with her brother so effortlessly made my heart ache. I missed being with them at home. I missed making her breakfast and hearing her imaginative stories. The guilt of missing out on Lorren's life was showing itself. I couldn't and didn't want to leave Dominic, but in that moment, I wished I could be in two places at once.

As a measure of relief set in, my body became more aware of what I'd been putting it through the past several days. My back was sore, and my muscles were fatigued. And no amount of water and smoothies could replace rest and meals. I decided that instead of spending another night in a recliner, I'd call my friend Jen, who lived about ten minutes away from the hospital. I asked her if I could sleep on her couch for a few hours that night, before returning to the hospital around five or six in the morning. She agreed and encouraged me to come by earlier so that I could get a full night's rest: "He has twenty-four-hour nursing support, so now is the time to rest, if you can." She was right and I knew it.

A couple of hours later, I got a text from her: *Okay, don't be mad, but I thought about it, and I booked you a hotel room across the street so you don't have to travel all the way to my place. You can walk and be at the bedside in three minutes. This way you can go back and forth throughout the night if you want. I also got a room with two beds, so that if your parents or Lorren decide they want to stay overnight, they can.*

I was taken aback by her generosity. Truth be told, I hadn't even thought about a hotel, and our budget wouldn't have sustained it anyway. Parking every day plus food for Paul and a smoothie for me was starting to add up, and it hadn't even been a week yet. Our friends and family had been sending Starbucks gift cards, which I was immensely thankful for, and I'd been blowing through them quickly.

Are you kidding me? I replied. *WHY?!* I tried to get Jen to agree to let me pay for at least part of the room, but she refused. *Wow, if you really didn't want me to sleep on your couch, you should have said so—you didn't have to get a hotel room!* I teased, falling back on a defense mechanism I use frequently: humor.

Paul and I talked it over, and since we'd had to cancel the family vacation to Florida, which was supposed to happen in less than a week, we decided to take Lorren to the hotel for the day, let her sleep there with us overnight, and then when I headed back to Dominic's bedside in the morning, Paul would go swimming or do something else fun in the hotel with Lorren so she'd feel special.

It was hard for me to leave the hospital walls that night. It would be my first time stepping outside. But with encouragement from the nurse, who promised that Dominic would be well taken care of (and would likely be asleep the entire time), I headed across the street to the hotel. I slept for five hours straight that night, which was more than I had in a week. As soon as I woke up, I left to be with Dominic, feeling nervous because no one had called me with an update. There he was, sleeping soundly, hugging his teddy-bear blanket.

I don't think Jen knows just how much that hotel room did for Paul, Lorren, and me. It allowed me to spend a night with my daughter for the first time in a week, and our family of four was able to be together for almost a whole day. Thank you isn't enough, but it was all I could think to say to her.

ANOTHER MRI

From Tuesday onward, Dominic started to become more alert and agitated, particularly when being examined by the doctors. *I'd be cranky too*, I thought, *if I were being poked and prodded all day every day for reasons I didn't understand.* It was difficult to get him to sleep in the evenings, and since I couldn't rock him in my arms due to the IV and arterial lines, I had to sing/coo and stroke his head to try to settle him. The neurologists thought the agitation was a great sign of recovery. They told me he had good sensory reactions when they touched his left leg, and some reaction when they touched his left arm. They were impressed that he could feel anything at all. I felt that was promising and was cautiously optimistic as to what the next MRI results would show.

When Wednesday arrived, Paul and I were nervous. Since Monday night, we'd been receiving all good news. But after something so bad and rare, how could it all go well? Still, we did our best to remain confident. Dominic attempted to smile at us for the first time that day—an adorable half smile. The left side of his face didn't move a millimeter, and his eye was wide open, but it was a smile nonetheless. The physiotherapist came by and massaged his arm and leg and taught me how to do passive range-of-motion exercises, which involved moving his body in certain ways so that he wouldn't get stiff from lack of motion.

The MRI took place around 4:00 p.m. Lorren and my parents were at the hospital, and we played with Lorren in the PICU waiting room while it was happening. My father ended up running into an old colleague who was visiting a family member, reminding me that the world wasn't as big as it seemed.

At 5:30 p.m., Paul and I left my parents and Lorren in the waiting room and returned to Dominic's bedside wondering if we'd have to wait until the next day to get the results, since it was late in the day. Thankfully, the neurology fellow explained that although the radiologist hadn't completed their report, the preliminary findings were in: no bleeding in the brain, blood had begun flowing to the affected parts of the brain, indicating that the clot was beginning to dissipate, and the swelling hadn't gotten any worse.

Paul started to cry, and I turned to the doctor and asked in a quiet voice, "Are you saying that the worst is over now?"

She smiled and replied softly, "Yes, I would say it is."

A tidal wave of relief washed over me. I started to cry the happiest, fullest tears I'd ever cried before. The doctor's eyes began to well up, too, and I thanked her so much for all her work and for taking the time to talk to us that evening instead of waiting until the next day.

All the tension and strength I'd been using to hold myself up seemed to come out in those tears. I felt looser, calmer, and more at ease. Dominic was beside us sleeping away, unaware of the monumental news we'd just received. I cried again when we told our parents and Lorren. My mom and I hugged, and Paul explained to my dad what the doctor had said.

Lorren immediately brought us back to reality: "Mommy, don't cry. Dominic's going to be okay! Now we have to hurry, or the restaurant is going to close!" We'd told Lorren we'd take her to the restaurant across the street for dinner.

Nothing like a two-year-old to keep it real.

NEUROPLASTICITY—THE BASICS

Neuroplasticity is a topic I knew very little about at the time of Dominic's stroke, but I soon learned that knowledge of it can be helpful to anyone looking to grow and develop—it's not just relevant to people who have brain injuries.

Neuroplasticity is the concept that the brain isn't hardwired permanently, but rather is like plastic and can be molded and remolded over and over, which looks like learning, relearning, and adapting. Children's brains are even more moldable than adults' brains because they're physically developing. Dominic's brain had lost some of itself to the stroke but could still learn and attain skills using other areas. It just had to learn to be more efficient in how it assigned tasks.

The brain has two hemispheres: the left and the right. Each is responsible for different functions. For those who are right-handed, the left hemisphere is generally the dominant side. The left houses the communication center and a lot of the cognitive function.

Think of the brain as real estate. Different areas of the brain are plots of land earmarked for future developments—e.g., physical movement and sensation, pattern recognition, memory, balance, coordination, etc. At the time of Dominic's stroke, over 33 percent of his brain's real estate flooded, and it couldn't be restored. This sounds scary, and it absolutely is. The beauty here is there are many empty lots available in the brain. Lots for which there are permits in place but on which construction hasn't yet begun. An area that might normally house one function could learn to house two, or even numerous functions, if trained efficiently. Learning this was so helpful for me.

As recently as fifty years ago, it was believed that after a brain injury, whatever was lost was gone for good. We now know that skills and abilities can be relearned both physically and cognitively, with few exceptions. This is especially true in younger brains.

If the brain were hardwired, Dominic's future would look bleak. The changes in him between the time of his stroke and now, five years later, are astounding. The brain has this level of learning potential that so few people are able to tap into. And the more it learns, the more its capacity to learn grows. You can relearn and relocate functions with an acquired brain injury—it just takes a lot of work.

This isn't specific to brain injury. Neuroplasticity is very much a part of my work as a mental-health clinician, too. Take negative thought patterns. If you live life thinking, *I'm not good enough*, for example, you create a negative story that's pervasive. The brain builds an "I'm not good enough" lens through which information is filtered and understood. Positives become minimized and the mistakes, trip-ups, and unfortunate events are highlighted to fit the story. When you challenge that thought and realize that you are, in fact, good enough, and practice this, the story can become positive. Self-confidence can grow. New lenses form and become stronger. In order for us to be able to change our minds and adapt, our brain has to create new neuropathways—a brain map, so to speak.

The same applies to anxious thoughts. *Something bad is going to happen.* This thought, if repeated often enough, creates a chain reaction that has neurological effects. The neurons responsible for this thought become stronger and stronger, creating a brain map telling us to continue thinking *Something bad is going to happen.* Over time, it becomes as automatic as breathing. We don't have to THINK the thought—it just shows up. If we acknowledge this and intentionally change the thought, come up with a more neutral or positive one, eventually the anxious thought becomes less pervasive. That's because new neuropathways form, providing much-needed relief from that intense anxiety. Like a brain injury, the anxiety doesn't necessarily go away; we just become better equipped to manage the symptoms.

Unhealthy coping or thought patterns can become habits. Habits don't form overnight, and they don't change overnight either. Change is slow. It ebbs and flows. There are setbacks and challenges and periods of complete remission. Changing how we think about healing is important. It's not a linear journey.

The neuroplasticity that gave me immense hope about Dominic's recovery is the same neuroplasticity that gave me immense hope about my own recovery. Change happens whether we think about it or not. We're not the same people we were a year ago, and we'll be different a year from now. We can always learn and grow from experiences if we're open to doing so. It's what we do with this learning and how we acknowledge our growth that makes the difference when it comes to our happiness and positivity.

LIVING IN A HOSPITAL—A TRAUMA

On Thursday, February 1, six days after we arrived at the PICU, Dominic was moved to the neurology unit. I had to count the number of days we'd been in the hospital a few times because it felt more like sixty. Had it really been less than a week?

The doctors had started Dominic on a twice-daily dose of a blood thinner called enoxaparin by injection and removed the continuous IV of heparin. The EEG probes had been removed, and he also no longer needed the arterial line. He was starting to look like some new version of himself. Just one IV and the NG tube remained—an incredible improvement from the week before.

We moved to the fifth floor, where we were set up in a private room. I now had a vinyl cot to sleep on and a private bathroom. Paul brought Dominic a few toys to play with in his crib, which he did with his right hand.

Shortly after starting to play, he appeared to realize his left side wasn't working. To prevent him from getting frustrated, I placed the toys on his right side and elevated the crib, since he could no longer sit up on his own. Using his right hand and foot, he continued playing with the toys, pushing buttons, moving things around, etc. Paul almost got a laugh out of him that day. He was starting to smile a few times per day, and at one point he smiled so big it almost crossed the halfway point.

When gazing outwards, Dominic's eyes always veered to the right. This was a symptom of the brain injury and possibly meant vision loss. After a few days in the neurology unit, Dominic was able to get his eyes to midline for a few seconds at a time when something really caught his attention. We saw small changes each day, and these changes taught me how neuroplasticity works. New neuropathways were being created. He was relearning how to do things. It almost looked like magic. My hope started to grow with each half smile, each attempt to move, each eye shift.

While Dominic napped, I'd either write in my journal or walk around trying to remind myself of life outside his hospital room. I'd wander the halls of 5C, where some children were completely bedridden. Some looked to be in a state similar to Dominic's, while others were much more mobile. Outside the unit were patients at the hospital for a variety of reasons: cancer, orthopedic issues, mental health, etc. People came from far and wide for treatment at this world-class hospital.

I remember walking down the hall passing other parents looking the way I felt—sleep deprived, terrified, and confused. Some looked numb, angry, or weepy. It wasn't easy seeing other sick children and their parents going through their medical journeys. Many parents looked worn down, somber, and tense. But some laughed and smiled. Which one was I, I wondered? I wanted to be the latter, offering hope and happiness to my child and family, but I knew that I was a mix of them all. We all were. Every minute was different.

When I finally looked in a mirror one morning, I barely recognized myself. My skin looked as if it had aged about ten years in less than two weeks. My hair hadn't been brushed, and I hadn't even asked Paul to bring me shampoo and conditioner. I just used baby soap to wash my body and hair. I wore the same nursing tank tops with whatever sweater I had to layer on top. My pants were starting to feel looser. One day I stared out the window at the skyscrapers and the snow-topped cars and sidewalks and thought about how I'd missed out on a few big snowfalls by staying indoors. I would have happily shoveled snow daily if it meant my child didn't have to experience this, or my daughter didn't have to adjust to life with an absent mother. Those thoughts spent a few minutes in my head, and then I chose to refocus on healing.

Every night Paul would go home to put Lorren to bed. Once Dominic started spending some time out of bed during the days, I tried to emulate our normal bedtime routine as much as possible. He slowly started to remember how to self-soothe and rest in bed without making a fuss. I was so proud of him. Then I'd attempt to fall asleep, but a lot of times this didn't happen, no matter how tired I was. The nights were the hardest. I'd hear the machines and other patients or staff talking. One night all I could hear was a girl screaming at the top of her lungs: "STOP! STOP! NO! I DON'T WANT IT! PLEASE STOP!" My heart broke. No matter how stellar the staff are, this is a place no parent wants their child to be. I was so grateful that Dominic was young during this ordeal. I hoped he and Lorren would never remember this time in our lives, that they wouldn't have to bear the brunt of remembering this trauma, as Paul and I would.

Living in a hospital is a surreal experience. It's a sterile, cold (or hot), dry, loud (even when it's quiet), and at times chaotic. You can hear crying, soft conversations, arguments, and beeps of machinery from adjoining rooms. And it's full of very intense emotions. Even after Dominic was discharged, I continued to hear the beeping of machines. I'd close my eyes at night and hear faint cries and screams, remember the nurses' chatter, etc. It's as if those memories became etched in my brain. I could also smell SickKids for weeks after we left—the cleaners, the disinfectants, the detergent for the bedsheets.

It's weird how quickly it started to feel normal, though. During the hours in the day when Dominic napped, I'd put a sign on the door saying he was asleep (this didn't stop people from walking in and waking him up, but it was my attempt to minimize disruption) and then journal or watch a movie on TV. I moved more slowly than I was used to. In some ways it was less busy than being at home with a two-and-a-half-year-old and a baby. I didn't have to cook, clean, organize, or come up with exciting games. I chose to focus on the gratitude I had for the people in my life who were picking up the pieces for me, both inside and outside the hospital walls.

This was our home. A home we didn't choose to live in. A home we wished we'd never need. And yet here we were, grateful to have access to this place.

Over time, the beeps, the flashing lights on the pumps and other machines, the call bell—it all became less jarring. The sounds even started to blend into the background. But the cries, the screams, the agitation . . . that never got easier to hear. There are certain aspects of hospital living I don't think I'll ever forget.

As traumatic as a hospital can be, it's also where bonds are made faster than anywhere else. In a rehabilitation hospital, the lengths of stays tend to be longer, providing the opportunity for communal eating and recreation. Almost like summer camp: a place where no one knows anyone else. Everyone is out of their comfort zone and thrust into small living quarters with people from all over the province. Many of these people have little in common. But in a children's hospital one thing is unanimous: everyone is there for their kids.

The hospital is a place where camaraderie lives. Parents there have a mutual understanding of the terrifying earthquake comprised of the medical emergencies and/or surgeries, the what-ifs of waiting, the tests, the quick learning involved in a new diagnosis and treatment plan, and the making of life-or-death decisions for your child. No matter what unique circumstance brings you to a neurology floor, you're dealing with the brain. Few people outside of this circle can truly understand. We and the other parents were bonded by our traumas.

Trauma is a prolonged emotional and/or psychological response that often results from living through (or witnessing) a distressing event. Post-traumatic stress disorder is characterized by flashbacks, nightmares, and vivid memories that become intrusive and pervasive. It's difficult to move forward, and to cope. Fear, shame, and a sense of powerlessness often set in. Certain sounds, smells, sights, or physical sensations can trigger the flashbacks. The emotion felt during a flashback is as raw and intense as it was the day it occurred. Sometimes even more so.

Divorce rates are higher for couples who have had children stay in the NICU/PICU for an extended amount of time. This makes sense, as people cope in different ways. Some talk it out, others shut down. Some use distraction, avoidance, or denial. Different coping styles, coupled with exhaustion, stress, and fear, can drive a wedge between a couple. If a child and family are living with long-term effects after a stay, the stress can become too much to bear. The weight of the worry and added responsibilities can crack even a solid foundation. My own marriage experienced challenges and change because of what we went through.

Watching my baby lie on a gurney, swollen, with a dozen tubes coming out of every hole in his body and being unable to hold him, cradle him, *cure* him—it cut my heart more than any knife could. The memory of those early days makes me weep even as I type this. Looking at his innocent face, I'd wonder what the hell happened. What was coming? Would he get through it? Would he survive? If he survived, would he have any quality of life? Which would be worse? The constant questions and the fear were paralyzing. And yet, he looked peaceful. My cooing, singing, and stroking of Dominic's hair weren't just about soothing him but also me. I couldn't take his place, but I could hold the memories for him and work toward making sense of them, even if it took me forever. I vowed to do just that, in hopes that he wouldn't have to.

Nearly losing our child and then navigating a brand-new world of raising a child with special needs changed me to my core. I have learned that although I can feel pain, anguish, fear, and worry in deeper ways than I could have imagined, I can also feel love, happiness, joy, and relief in deeper ways too. That's the interesting thing about this experience—the intensity of the darkness helped me to appreciate the light.

I have learned so much about resilience, strength, and adaptability.

FOUR

Nonmedical Challenges

SICK CHILD + SIBLINGS

Anything can become normal to children. Whenever Lorren visited the hospital, she was well behaved and enjoyed spending time with Dominic and us. She never complained about going home. The tubes, the lack of movement, the facial droop—she didn't care. She wanted to kiss her brother and show him the pictures she'd drawn, as usual. The love was constant, and their bond was clear. She was a dream toddler. She remains an amazing sister.

One Sunday evening when Lorren and Paul dropped Dominic and me off at the rehabilitation hospital, where we spent a few months after our stay at the acute-care hospital (more on this later), her wisdom shone through. As Lorren and Paul said goodbye and turned to leave, I kept a smile on my face, even though I wanted to cry. I missed her so much, and I was dealing with how much guilt I felt about her being cared for by someone other than me. When Dominic first went into the hospital, Lorren wasn't going to daycare. She was with me at home 24/7. Paul later told me that as they walked away, Lorren said, "Daddy, it makes me sad that Mommy is all alone." Talk about insight. How could she even think of others at that age? Maybe she was thinking of herself too, being without Mom.

When Dominic and I returned home from the rehab hospital and settled into our new normal, however, things with Lorren changed. Defiance set in; tantrums skyrocketed. She went from sleeping ten hours a night to waking up two to four times, just because. She'd say she wanted snuggles, or that she didn't want to sleep. I quickly became exhausted and angry. Unable to see what she was doing, I complained to Paul one day about my fatigue and anguish over the fact that she was no longer sleeping through the night. As I said the words out loud, it dawned on me: the pendulum was swinging. During the crisis, Lorren knew things weren't right. She saw us cry, she heard the fear and exhaustion in our voices. She stayed quiet. She compensated.

Once we were back, she demanded the attention she desperately needed and, frankly, deserved. She was expressing her innate need for bonding and connection. One day, my therapist looked at me as I described our "no sleeping in our bed" rule and said, "Who cares about the rules? She wants a snuggle, give her a snuggle." Truthfully, the type A, rigid rule follower in me hadn't even thought of this. SO much in our life had changed, and I'd thought I was getting good at going with the flow, yet I met this change with resistance over and over (and still do sometimes). In the interest of self-growth and progress, I started to lie with her in her bed for a few extra minutes in the evening and soon noticed that doing this, even for four or five minutes, translated to fewer tantrums and less defiance the next day. She started waking less frequently at night, and when she did, I'd take her back to her room and, instead of tucking her in and kissing her head, I'd lie beside her. Even if I was tired. This wasn't easy in the beginning. I had to change my mindset and tell myself, *She's not acting out to make me angry. She's starved for attention. Attention she's entitled to.* We would never get back the time together that we'd lost, but I could help her to feel secure in her attachment. I needed this extra time together too. I needed to let go of the arbitrary rules I'd created and just be in the moment.

From her point of view, throughout Dominic's ordeal, all our focus appeared to be on him. We were at his bedside every day. I would talk about strokes, hemiplegia, epilepsy, rehabilitation, potential learning disabilities, assistive devices, etc. all the time. She heard it. What message did this send to her? She was ALWAYS on my mind, but I didn't talk about this to nearly the same degree. *How is she managing this?* I'd wonder. *Will this time apart ruin our relationship? Will we as a family be able to recover from this? How do I help her understand how much I love and care about her when on the surface it may not appear that I do?*

What happened was unfair to Dominic, but it was also incredibly unfair to Lorren. She didn't deserve it. Her parents were gone for weeks. Her brother was gone for months. And when he did return, her parents and everyone who visited focused on Dominic's progress and changes. Soon after I returned home, Paul and I made a point of bringing Lorren into conversations. I'd talk about her in a positive way when speaking to others. If I was talking to a therapist about Dominic and Lorren was around, I'd mention what a great sister he had—a sister who was showing him all she could do so that he could learn from her. If family talked about Dominic's progress, I'd respond and then tell them about a new skill Lorren had acquired or a beautiful art piece she'd made. I did this whether I thought she could hear me or not. The point was that I wanted to be deliberate in acknowledging that she was thought of, cared for, valued, and loved. Ultimately, I believe this strengthened our connection. It also set an example for our family and friends, showing them that we wanted Lorren included in conversations about our family and the healing journey. After all, it has impacted all of us.

What I've come to realize over the years is that kids don't need that much time with parents in terms of quantity. They need QUALITY time.

Many months after Dominic's stroke, during a medically unstable time (again, more to come on this), I had a discussion with her during some alone time together. I told her how unfair it must look, seeing her brother get so much attention.

Lorren, five years old at the time, replied, "You don't love me anymore. You only love Dominic and that's why you take care of him so much."

Rather than get defensive, as I would have done a few years earlier, I chose to validate her feelings. "I can see why you would think that," I said. "It must seem like we love him more because he gets so much more attention than you do, and because we have to give him medicine and because we take him to so many appointments." She agreed. Then I asked Lorren for her advice. "What could Mommy and Daddy do to show you how much we love you?"

Her advice was brilliant. "You can give me a hug before we eat." Easy-peasy. I started doing this immediately and saw positive effects on her within twenty-four hours. After the "lunchtime hug" the next day, she pranced off and sang, "Mommy loves me, Mommy loves me." Children know what they need—more so than we give them credit for. It often isn't as complicated as we adults make it (or is it just me?).

There's no question this experience affected our daughter in ways we likely don't know about yet. She knows more about neurological specialties, brain anatomy, and therapeutic techniques than most children her age. Her level of empathy and her caregiving abilities are far beyond her years. We try to avoid any parentification, but we catch her encouraging her brother to "use lefty" and congratulating him when he tries a new movement or recognizes a shape/color/sequence. She's his biggest cheerleader and teacher. This experience has shaped a part of her personality forever. Her soul is beautiful, and she continues to amaze us with her brilliance, empathy, and gentle encouragement. We are very lucky.

GUILT

During the twenty-week ultrasound when I was pregnant with my daughter, the day we were going to find out the baby's gender, I was convinced we were having a boy. I'd always envisioned myself with sons, though I'm not sure why. When the technician said it was a girl, I asked how accurate the test was.

The tech said, "I'm about eighty percent sure. Honestly, mothers know best, and most of the time, whatever the mother thinks the baby is, they're right."

Throughout the rest of the pregnancy, when people talked about "her," I'd say, "Or him." And when Lorren arrived, following a twenty-five-hour labor, I was a bit surprised. My "mother's intuition" had been wrong. I felt like a failure from the start.

I was diagnosed with postpartum mood disorder (anxiety) after Lorren was born. I couldn't leave her; I couldn't sleep if she was awake with someone else watching her. I worried she wasn't attached to me. No matter what I did I was nervous, anxious about making a mistake or something bad happening to her. When Lorren was eleven weeks old, Paul and I went to the wedding of one of his good friends. My parents babysat. The entire drive there, I was in full-blown panic mode telling him to drive more carefully because I'd had a vision of us being killed in a car accident. I was petrified we'd leave our newborn baby orphaned. The fear was so intense it felt as if I were choking.

Part of my brain was aware that these types of thoughts weren't realistic. I'd say that they were ridiculous, and I employed cognitive behavioral therapy strategies without any self-compassion. I'd fact-check, evaluate evidence, and then berate myself for thinking and feeling a certain way. I knew that the likelihood of something bad happening was minute, yet the fear made it feel as if it were guaranteed. Chastising myself for thinking these thoughts only fueled my guilt and shame instead of allowing me to let go of them.

Mother's intuition is something I'd always thought was innate. I'd believed that the answers would just come to me, and they'd be right.

As I embarked on the journey of motherhood, I began to realize that anxiety is sneaky. Anxiety seems very similar to a "gut feeling"—turns out it's usually just the crippling fear of making a mistake. After about six months of therapy and life experience with Lorren, I calmed and began getting into a groove. I could go out without crying or having hysterical thoughts run through my brain. I started to appreciate the time at the grocery store and the rare occasion out with a friend.

I didn't want to teach my children maladaptive coping techniques or fear-fueled responses to everyday decisions and challenges, so once the dust settled on new-mom life, I really began to work on myself through therapy, meditation, and exercise.

My taking care of myself directly affects how I take care of my children. More than once, I've lost myself along this path, but every time I emerge from the cloud of anxiety, I realize that I was the answer all along. Focusing on my health and well-being always has a positive impact on my parenting abilities.

When Dominic had his stroke, the mom guilt came back like a boomerang straight to the face. HOW could I not have known something was wrong immediately? Sure, he was seven and a half months old and had been teething for weeks. But that cry. It sounded so different after a certain point. I hadn't even known babies had strokes, yet I took on the blame wholeheartedly.

As mentioned, I took a photo of him sleeping in my bed early that fateful morning, and for years it was a reminder of my most epic failure. Whenever the guilt started to ramp up, I'd look at it—a form of emotional self-harm, perhaps. A big step in my healing was deleting that picture.

The post-traumatic stress I experienced as a result of the day of his stroke created an association between relaxing moments—e.g., watching TV with Lorren and enjoying the slow pace of the morning—and something terrible happening. The guilt associated with "letting my guard down" is something I must challenge daily. It's an automatic response.

Watching your child nearly die evokes the deepest sense of helplessness. I felt as if I were in a fog, yet I remember so many details. It also now feels like a different lifetime. Certain memories make me feel as if I'm watching someone else. In the aftermath, when I thought back to the early days—lack of sleep, intense emotions, the hard work to remain positive and embody healing energy—the guilt crept up. *I should have woken him up sooner. I should have known the cry was more serious than teething pain. I should have had that mother's intuition.* And the guilt quickly turned to shame.

After the stroke, I spoke with the physicians investigating what could have caused it. I told them that in the first three months of Dominic's life, I wasn't producing enough breastmilk. I'd seen pediatricians, lactation consultants, and a physician who specialized in breastfeeding, and they'd all told me to take the supplements and prescription medication that would increase milk supply. I drank the water, I ate the oatmeal and lactation cookies, I took the fenugreek, blessed thistle, domperidone, etc. I'd breastfeed then pump to increase stimulation. None of it was enough.

Dominic was eight and a half pounds when he was born, and by three months old he was just over ten pounds. His diapers were wet and he was growing, but too slowly. I finally saw a third lactation consultant, who gently touched my shoulder and said, "Stop trying to be a hero.

Supplement with formula." She explained that it didn't have to be all or nothing. I could do both. She was the first one to say that. Everyone else said that the more I bottle-fed, the less milk I'd have and the less he'd want it. I was able to breastfeed for another eight months after that with supplementation. He started to grow immediately. And as happy as it made me to see him flourish, I felt ashamed that I hadn't listened the 1,200 times my mother told me to give him a bottle of formula and instead listened to the "professionals" who were strangers.

When I finally opened that brochure on pediatric stroke, a few days after we received it, I read that one of the causes of stroke is dehydration. That was it. It *had* been my fault. I went straight to the conclusion that I had no real evidence to go to. I'd done this to him. Every doctor told me that it wasn't possible. Not at his age, not at that time. Not this type of stroke. Paul even searched "stroke caused by dehydration" and said that these types of strokes aren't the same. None of this data mattered. The emotional hold I had on my shame was too strong. Everyone was wrong. I was responsible for my children and therefore I was responsible for what happened. And for this, I'd never be forgiven. Like a captain on a sinking ship, I was going down with it.

If I'd woken him sooner, maybe the damage would have been reversible. The infarct in the brain would have been treated sooner and maybe he wouldn't have been left with permanent disabilities. Maybe he would have recovered fully. Maybe he wouldn't have developed epilepsy. I lived in these *maybes* for a while

Doctors told me that if I'd taken him to the hospital earlier, before his state of consciousness changed, they would have sent me home and said he was teething. They told me if I'd waited longer, he likely would have died. "You brought him in at the perfect time," they said, trying to console me. Something I was sure they told most parents consumed with guilt and self-loathing. It took me a long time to start believing that there could be a scenario in which I wasn't entirely responsible.

The guilt spilled into every aspect of caregiving and life. I can't stop Dominic from being poked and prodded in the hospital. Guilt. I can't explain what's happening in a way that he understands. Guilt. I'm tired out from needing to rearrange my schedule to fit in appointments. Guilt. Dominic requires orthotics to walk, and he needs therapy multiple times a week while other kids are off learning taekwondo or soccer. Guilt.

I sometimes catch myself going into "snowplow" parenting mode—I want to plow all the problems out of the way, so my kids have no challenges. This is not the parent I want to be, though. That doesn't build resiliency. I don't want my kids to go through life never experiencing challenges; I want them to be able to overcome them. To learn and grow. In order for them to learn that, I have to do it for myself.

While I no longer burst into rageful tears every time I think of my part in that day, I still feel it from time to time. I've had to work hard on self-compassion and forgiveness over the years. Most days are filled with joy, and I'm proud of how far we've all come. I know now that I didn't cause his stroke. When I see my child struggle with something that a neurotypical child would do with ease, it's a painful reminder of what happened. It's also a reminder to fight the automatic tendency to blame myself or focus on the negative. Sometimes it feels like a full-time job to keep it at bay. Over time, though, it gets easier.

The nature of my anxiety makes me an overprotective parent. I worry about most things. I worry about my level of worry. How will it affect my children? Am I exhibiting anxious behavior? Are they going to grow up to do the same? Part of that worry is fueled by lack of control. Anxiety loves question marks. It thrives on them. The more uncertainty there is in my world, the more anxiety can create scenarios that spark fear, anguish, confusion, and chaos.

Working on relinquishing control has been my most difficult challenge. It's also the most important one. In the moment, a crisis is terrifying. It's also an OPPORTUNITY. A catapult to change and growth. Nothing gives us the chance to learn faster, and grow further, than a crisis. As a serial goal setter, I always strive to improve myself. Challenging experiences help me do just that. We don't have to embrace and like what's happening. But we can accept what is and trust the process. It's tough, but so worth it.

I've learned the importance of self-forgiveness and compassion. I no longer beat myself up for needing a break. The guilt still tugs at my heart, but I've come to understand that part of that is a cognitive story I've had on repeat for decades. It's an old habit. I'm working to rewrite the story of me. Trauma and challenge offer the chance to do this kind of work, and for that I'm thankful. Without these experiences, I wouldn't be on the path I'm currently on.

LEARNING TO COPE

In a crisis, I'm a doer. I like to help when things get messy—it gives me a sense of control within the chaos. This is how I stay levelheaded. The sense of control (even if false) gives me a reprieve from the anxiety. Before Dominic had his stroke, my anxiety was triggered whenever a plan changed, or something unexpected occurred, and it would present itself as me being nitpicky, bossy, demanding, rude, angry. All a façade to mask my desperation to regain perceived control.

When Dominic had his stroke, I quickly became the director of affairs. I made a logistical plan to get to the hospital, arranged childcare for my daughter, organized what needed to be packed, figured out who should drive, etc. But once we were on this journey for longer, I realized there were unknowns that I couldn't plan my way out of. There was nothing I could do but hold on to hope. I had to trust the process. I could no longer plan my way calm. And I had to rely on others to pick up the pieces outside of that hospital room.

Letting people help isn't always easy. Everyone has their own way of doing things, and the expectations and routine I'd spent years creating for my daughter changed. We lost the consistency we'd built. It was a hard pill to swallow.

As mentioned, Paul and I didn't allow visitors in the ICU during those first touch-and-go hours because we wanted to protect the energy around Dominic. We also didn't want people to see him this way in case it was the last time they saw him. I didn't even consider that people would come to the hospital to care for Paul or me. When a couple of my cousins met us in the lobby one day, I apologized for not inviting them to the bedside. One of my cousins said, "Dominic won't remember this. I'm here for you." It hadn't dawned on me until then that people would want to support us—after all, we weren't ill. I didn't know how to accept this support.

The text messages, phone calls, food dropped off, positive thoughts, good vibes, and prayers that people sent were incredible. In a time when I was feeling disconnected from faith, having others pray on my behalf was a true gift. It carried us through such a challenging time. Letting people help was a critical factor in our making it through those days. I wish I'd been more open about the crippling guilt back then. I didn't talk about it with anyone other than Paul and the doctors.

In the beginning, I believed I wasn't coping. I was in survival mode. I didn't knowingly call on the cognitive behavioral therapy strategies that I so often use to help clients reframe negative situations. The only thing that I was able to use, especially in those first seventy-two hours, was the healing-light visualization. I'd sit still, hold Dominic's hand or forehead, and picture healing light engulfing him, cradling him in a way I would have done if I'd been allowed to hold him. I did this several times a day. I also visualized his brain healing as he slept. While stroking his hair slowly, I pictured holding him. I sang his favorite lullaby for hours and repeated, "You're so strong, so brave, and you're doing so well." I said this fifty or more times a day. Now that I think about it, maybe I was manifesting this truth in myself too.

We internalize what's in our environment. That's why I was adamant about saying positive things around Dominic and giving myself space if I needed to go to a darker place. Paul and I needed the opportunity to sit with the dark moments when they arrived. The brain is powerful and truly amazing. Sometimes it takes care of us without our realizing it. It took me writing this paragraph to realize that's what happened in my experience.

The social worker version of me would point out that the things I did in those moments WERE coping strategies. I sat with the negative emotions. I wrote them down. I pictured the darkest images. Then, I chose to focus on the positive. When the catastrophizing crept in, I acknowledged it and then tried to challenge it. The only things missing in this picture were self-compassion and self-validation, which are critical to processing and healing.

I often reminded myself of where I was—with some of the best health-care professionals around who specialized in pediatric stroke. I told myself and my family we were going to be okay, even though I didn't know if it were true.

It is true.

Even in the darkest moments, where there isn't a glimmer of light in sight, the capacity to heal is there. The smallest of changes, the smallest of improvements, the smallest of movements—it's all progress.

FIVE

Making Progress

About ten days poststroke, I asked the occupational therapist (OT) if Dominic could try eating something orally, since he'd thoroughly enjoyed it before. I didn't like the idea of him having an NG tube long term—I worried that he'd dislodge it, that it would get infected or misplaced in his abdomen/intestine, or worse. The OT agreed to try pureed foods in tiny quantities. The first time we tried it, Dominic was falling asleep and cranky. It was unsuccessful. The second time was the same. We scheduled the third time for the end of a nap, so that he'd be refreshed and hopefully ready to start using the left side of his mouth for the first time since arriving. I did my best to remain hopeful that doing an enjoyable activity might help spark his memory of what it was like to eat, and in turn, jump-start connections in his brain to get that side of his face working again. Muscle memory helps.

When the OT arrived, I felt nervous and excited for Dominic. I was afraid that he'd choke on what we gave him yet hopeful this could be a breakthrough in his progress. I placed a small amount of food on a spoon (about the size of a pea). Dominic looked at it, and his eyes made it clear: he wanted it. Unfortunately, his mouth couldn't figure out how to interpret that message. He attempted to open his mouth, which was slanted, and tried to stick out his tongue, which was also at an angle. He tried to lick the food from the spoon, but he didn't seem to know how.

I felt fear rise in my chest but swallowed it down. *It takes time*, I told myself. *He can do this.* The OT assured me this was common and that it could take some time for Dominic to relearn how to eat. She told me to look for the following stress signs during taste stimulations: coughing, wet sound in voice, eyes watering/widening, fingers stretched, nasal flaring. These were indicators of choking. The idea that Dominic could silently aspirate was terrifying.

Part of me thought, *Forget it, let the professionals do it. This is totally out of my wheelhouse.* Another part of me thought, *The professionals have caseloads of over twenty-five patients and likely won't be able to see him for more than a few minutes a day, if that.* I reminded myself that I was his mother. *I'm capable of teaching my child, just as I do at home.* The tasks and the strategies just had to change. I had to do things with more caution to keep him safe.

Little by little, a few times a day, Dominic and I tried one small sample of food. It was tough. With every lick or attempt at a munch, Dominic would get angry and cry. He wanted the food, but the muscles in his mouth were trying to refigure out what to do. The more agitated he became, the less we could work on it. Deciding we needed a change, I made the feeding into a game. I'd sing "Itsy Bitsy Spider" or "The Wheels on the Bus" and changed the scenery (he enjoyed being near the window). By the end of our hospital stay, four days later, Dominic was able to take pureed foods orally. I'd also slightly watered down the food with breastmilk. He still received his main meals of breastmilk and formula via the NG tube, but it was definitely a step in the right direction on the road to recovery.

Those first days, I saw how hard Dominic was working and how determined this little boy was. It fueled my hope and helped me to cheer him on and figure out a way to help him reach his goals. His perseverance nurtured my own strength. It gave me the energy to figure out a way to assist and advocate for him. The therapists at the hospital had mentioned the importance of bringing awareness to the affected side, so we'd put pureed food on his left hand, stickers on his left leg, a sock with a scrunchy toy on his left foot, and toys on his left side, to give him reasons to turn his head or even just shift his eyes past midline. There was still no movement on that side, and he wouldn't turn his head to the left, but we kept at it. Slow and steady.

Again, change doesn't happen quickly. It's not linear. Whenever things weren't going smoothly or I felt scared or discouraged, I'd remind myself that this was a marathon, not a sprint.

DR. MOM

Around this time, Paul and I asked when we could expect the transition to Holland Bloorview Kids Rehabilitation Hospital to take place. We were informed that Dominic would be transferred there within a few days (about two weeks after his stroke). Unfortunately, the rehab facility had an outbreak of the flu when he was to be transferred, and no one was being admitted. My initial thought was that we'd wait in the hospital until a bed became available. But the team quickly started talking about sending Dominic home to our care to wait for rehabilitation, since he was now medically stable and healing.

The flame of anxiety burned in my gut. The research that Paul and I were brave enough to do indicated that the first six months following a stroke were the most critical for rehabilitation. How would we help Dominic recover? I'd been doing passive range-of-motion activities with him daily to make sure he didn't get stiff, but these wouldn't help him progress. On top of that, I didn't know how to manage the NG tube. I'd already "let" this catastrophe happen—what if I made a mistake and did something wrong again?

I also felt fearful that if we left the hospital, there'd be no push to get him into rehabilitation. *If he's at home, he's not "taking up space at the hospital"*—a thought I recalled from my work with adults. Staff promised this wouldn't happen. I was assured that he'd remain at the same priority level, regardless of where he was waiting for a bed. But I had a hard time believing this due to my work experience in orthopedic surgery. Patients who cost the system money are taken first. Those making do in the community can wait—because they're making do. I didn't want my son to "make do." He had the opportunity to make GAINS.

The hospital provided Paul and me a forty-five-minute training session on how to maintain and insert an NG tube. I walked to this session with my stomach in knots. Of all the care needs our son was leaving the hospital with, this one scared me the most. The nurse explained the importance of testing pH levels in his stomach before each feed—we'd have to pull liquid out of the tube that went from his nose down to his stomach and test the pH balance to confirm the tube was in the right spot. She showed us how and got us to take turns practicing on a doll. Then she talked about what to do if the tube became dislodged and food got into places it shouldn't be, such as the lungs. I broke down. Through my sobs, I relayed how uncomfortable I felt inserting an NG tube. I cried about not being a trained professional. I didn't feel that trying something on a doll, ONCE, was enough training to send us home with this kind of responsibility. I was totally overwhelmed. I was starting to panic.

The nurse who received the brunt of my outburst reassured me we could do it and said that if we really felt we couldn't, we could take Dominic to an emergency room to have the tube reinserted. But she also explained that if we did take him in, he'd be the lowest priority at that time and we'd have to wait.

An electrician, Paul said he felt confident he could do it if I held Dominic still. "I run wires all day long—this is easy," he said jokingly, as I wept. I loved him a little more in that minute for making such a ridiculous reference. I'd been spending so much time and energy trying to be strong for him that I'd forgotten how good he was at doing that for me.

After that training, the physician said that we were ready to go home—that night. "We're absolutely not ready," I immediately replied. The doctor tried to reassure us that because Dominic could be carried, it wasn't a safety risk. But he couldn't hold his head up on his own. He couldn't sit up. He couldn't even roll over.

I retorted by saying I had JUST received training on managing his NG tube and hadn't set up or managed ANY of Dominic's feeds without assistance. Neither had we set up the house with his equipment or gotten confirmation that the pharmacy had his medications in stock. Thankfully, a nurse advocated for us to have time to practice his care more independently, and the doctor conceded. My anxiety remained sky high, but at least we'd bought a bit more time.

That night, I practiced taking pH levels before feeds to ensure the NG tube had been placed in his stomach correctly; I set up the feeds in their bags, hung them on the gravity IV pole, and adjusted the speed of the drip. Then, once the feed was finished, I cleaned the bag, flushed the tube, and prepared the next feed—a mix of breastmilk and formula. I prepared his antiseizure medication, blood thinner, and injections and did his range-of-motion exercises. Everything went well. But what if I didn't get an aspirate reading? What if the NG tube got dislodged or came up with vomit that went into his lungs? I was catastrophizing. I knew it. And this cognitive distortion exacerbates symptoms of anxiety.

I was already feeling as if I'd failed as a mother, and now I was to return home to the role with added responsibilities. Part of me knew that I'd manage the tasks and eventually it would feel easier. But in that moment, I felt as if I were out at sea, barely able to swim. As if one small wave could take me out forever.

Still, I kept learning. I learned how to prepare injections so that I could give them to Dominic at home. I'd practice on an orange, and a few times, Paul even let me practice on him with saline (which we later found out was a HUGE no-no in the hospital—woops, *sorry*). I wanted to be as prepared as I could be for my new responsibilities. Dominic was teaching me the true meaning of strength and bravery. Injecting my child twice a day, overseeing hugely sedative medications, and maintaining an NG tube—these tasks were scary and foreign. I felt overwhelmed and had a few breakdowns. But a small voice inside told me that in the future, I'd look back on these tasks as simple, everyday "mom" duties. People self-inject all the time. If Dominic could pull through this stroke and still be smiling, then I could certainly handle a little needle, some medical care, and rehabilitation, right?

It only took me about two days of practice with oranges and one day using my husband's arm (bless that man) to feel as if I could reluctantly try doing it on Dominic. A week in, I was doing it faster, and at times Dominic wouldn't even cry, depending on where the injection site was.

I never fully felt comfortable with the NG tube, but I was doing it. The feeds came and went, the tubes were flushed, bags cleaned, formula prepared, breastmilk pumped, meds put through, etc. Dominic tolerated it, and I saw each feeding as a hurdle I'd jumped. Something to celebrate. A small victory. Every injection was a little win. It never felt normal, but I started to gain confidence. It started to get a tiny bit easier. I reminded myself that I was lucky I could manage his care. I started to shift from negative, resistant thinking to acceptance. I started to think only about the current moment and a few hours ahead. Anything further was filled with question marks, and that was scary. Focusing on each day made things easier. The negativity lessened in intensity, and I became more comfortable.

Within four or five days of being back at home, I was in a rhythm. I still had my nervous moments, but each success offered more ammunition to keep going. I'd reached this new place between surviving and feeling normal. I had a strong sense that Dominic would eat by mouth very soon, as he did better and better at his oral trials each day. Soon, he might even be able to suck a bottle again. That would be a huge victory. A major sign of healing. I held on to hope.

GOING HOME

Our discharge day, a Thursday, was chaotic. Before we left, a professor wanted to examine Dominic in front of students, so they could learn, and Paul and I had to go to Holland Bloorview Rehab for a tour as well as prepare all the supports and equipment we'd need at home. We'd done as much as we could the day before, buying equipment, calling our local compounding pharmacy, and speaking with home-care services.

I'd barely slept the night before, having had a restless night full of nightmares that Dominic's name would disappear from the waiting list for rehabilitation and that I'd do something wrong in caring for him, such as give him too much medication or miss doses altogether. That afternoon, the care coordinator contacted me, wanting to schedule an OT assessment to be done in the home the following Monday or Tuesday.

She assured us this could be canceled if Dominic was already at Bloor-view. She went over everything and then asked if there was anything else she could help with.

I shared my trepidation about managing the NG feedings on my own, with no one to check my work or assess whether Dominic was doing well.

"I didn't know your son had an NG tube," she replied. "It's not in the paperwork."

I was annoyed and, frankly, a little pissed off when I heard that. *Falling through the cracks already*, I thought. I couldn't have been clearer about our needs. I tried to refocus and proceeded to advocate for nursing care. The care coordinator agreed to put in a referral for a nurse who'd come to our home every day to check Dominic's NG tube, and for an additional pediatric nurse who could provide an overall assessment of Dominic on Monday. I agreed to any and all services offered. The hospital's emergency room would be the last-resort backup plan.

We arrived home around five that evening, and my parents and in-laws were waiting for us with dinner. It was my first time returning to the house since leaving in the ambulance. I was terrified. I wasn't even sure I'd be able to sleep in my own bed again, since that's where Dominic had been when this all started. I wondered if I should sleep on the twin mattress in Dominic's room that my parents had been using. Not just to be closer to Dominic, but also to be as far away from my own bed as possible.

In a true dichotomy of emotions, as fearful as I was to return to "ground zero," I couldn't wait to be near Lorren again. I'd missed my little girl so much, and she'd shown so much maturity and resilience over the past two weeks. She articulated to family and friends in her own words what had happened and seemed to have a good understanding of why we were away. Every time she visited the hospital, she'd ask if Dominic was still "a little bit sick" and if I was coming home. Being honest and upfront with Lorren had been the best course of action when it came to helping her understand how much she meant to us and how unfair the situation was to her. We'd explained in an age-appropriate way that Dominic had a "boo-boo in the brain" (she knows now that it was a blood clot) that made his left side forget how to move and that he'd have to work on getting stronger, which could take a long time.

We used these conversations as a chance to reinforce what a great big sister Lorren was. She seemed very excited for us to return home so she could "teach" Dominic how to play with toys, sit up, roll over, and do all the things he needed to relearn.

That first evening, Lorren was a bit clingy with me, which I figured was to be expected. Dominic was overtired and overstimulated, and Paul and I were exhausted. Dominic was grumpy, I was a nervous wreck. Our negativity fed off each other. After Paul and I set up and completed his first successful at-home tube feed, it was time for bed. This meant it was time for my first solo injection. Paul accompanied me into Dominic's bedroom and helped me hold him down as Dominic continued to wail out of frustration and fatigue. We'd been alternating injection site locations to give his limbs a break. Tonight, it was his right leg.

Scared and exhausted, I injected him, and as I did, he moved his leg and the tiny, thin needle scratched him slightly. He cried harder and I lost it. I put pressure on the leg and hoped it would stop bleeding instantly, forgetting that he was on a high dose of blood thinner. Paul left the room to get a Band-Aid, and when he returned he found me fighting back sobs.

"What am I doing?" I cried. "I can't even give a tiny injection without hurting him. How am I going to do this?" Despite my distress, I was being as quiet as possible because I didn't want our parents or Lorren to hear us. Our parents were waiting in the living room, hanging around until the kids were in bed and, I suspect, to make sure we were alright. Truthfully, all Paul and I wanted was to be alone so that we could feel all the feels—to talk, plan, cry, be scared, and reconnect. We were so grateful to have the support and assistance, and we also wanted to be alone.

In that dark bedroom, while I held Dominic's leg, Paul gently grabbed my shoulders and said, "Hold it together for now, and when everyone leaves, and the kids are asleep, we'll sit on the couch and have a good cry together." And that's just what we did.

Dominic calmed after a moment or two, and thankfully after a minute the bleeding stopped. After that, we completed the bedtime routine and Dominic passed out with exhaustion. Lorren also fell asleep rather quickly. Our parents left, and then Paul and I sat on the couch together for the first time in two weeks. I asked him to take one more day off work, so that I could have some help around the house while I figured out how to do this. He agreed. We went to bed early—together for the first time in two weeks—and I slept more soundly than I thought, only waking up in a panic two or three times. Every time I checked on Dominic, he was sound asleep.

The worst might be over, I told myself. *Maybe light at the end of the tunnel is closer than I thought.*

BECOMING AN ADVOCATE

On one of our first nights in the neurology unit, the pharmacy forgot to send up the enoxaparin when it was due. Dominic needed the anti-coagulant in a timely fashion, otherwise his next dose could be affected. I immediately told the nurse, who was busy with other patients—this is the difference between ICU and a general floor. Once you're out of the ICU, there's no one-to-one nursing. Fifteen minutes later, I decided it was enough. It was time to speak up.

I went to the nurses' station and asked them to call the pharmacy to find out what the holdup was. I attempted to stay calm, but I could feel myself getting tenser as the moments passed. I was advocating for my child, who couldn't do it for himself. The medication was there within moments. *Maybe I do have some maternal instincts after all*, I thought.

The doctors and nurses often encouraged me and gave me positive feedback about my abilities as a caregiver. I later realized this was also an attempt to boost my confidence so that I'd feel prepared to leave the hospital as soon as possible. It's not lost on me how costly it is to have a patient in an acute-care hospital. Discharge planning had been part of my job for years. I'd been the person cheering patients and families on regarding functioning at home. I'd set up home care for individuals and provided resources for services in their area that could supplement that help.

From a logistical standpoint, it's important for patients to leave acute-care hospitals as soon as they're ready. It reduces the risk of getting or spreading infection, it's more comfortable at home for patients, and of course, it costs the system a lot less money. In a country with universal healthcare, the last thing I wanted was to be a drain on the system. Especially one I was so grateful for. That said, I didn't want to take my son home if there was a risk he'd fall through the cracks.

My time as a hospital social worker reminded me of the importance of advocating for patients to receive what they need, both inside the hospital walls and within the community. And so I vocalized my concerns about Dominic falling through the cracks of the system several times to different staff members, to ensure this was stated at rounds. I wanted the team to know that if Dominic was made to wait for a long period in the community, this could negatively impact his potential for recovery. In the hospital, he had access to occupational and physical therapy daily—this was something he wouldn't get in the community, and we couldn't afford to hire someone to come to our home daily. The hospital assured me that it would be a matter of days until Dominic got a bed offer.

Advocating for my child in a way that was articulate and professional but also conveyed urgency was absolutely exhausting. I'd feel a lump start to rise in my throat as I spoke, and there were times when my voice got shaky because I was so nervous and/or desperate to be heard and understood and validated. At times I worried that I was being a nuisance or asking for too much. At other times I worried that if I stayed silent, I'd crumble trying to take it all on. I requested a referral for community support—to have an occupational therapy assessment and nursing care in the home. This hadn't been offered to me, but when I explained why I felt it was important, the Local Health Integration Network (LHIN) care coordinator agreed to put in the referral.

After a decent first night's sleep, we all seemed to be in much better spirits, and I felt more optimistic about my ability to care for my family. I was less fearful about the injection that day, as the site was on his affected side, and he wouldn't be moving around as much when I did it. He barely flinched. It was a bit chaotic getting the medications and feeds ready before Dominic woke up and getting breakfast ready for Lorren so that I'd have time to test the tube placement and begin Dominic's feeding, but we made it work.

The anxiety of being home began dissipating. Dominic became comfortable quickly and loved being around his sister. Lorren loved having Dominic and me around too, which was comforting. Dominic was either in our arms, in his highchair, in a baby swing that he was a bit too big for, or propped up in the corner of the couch with pillows—not ideal for playing with toys, but with Lorren providing entertainment he seemed content.

The plan was for us to have someone from the LHIN come to the house the next day to check the NG tube and ensure that Dominic was doing well. I contacted the LHIN in the morning and spoke to the case worker to confirm what time someone was coming. She stated that nursing care was contracted out and she wasn't sure what time they'd come but that she'd left a voicemail for them. She said they'd call me back. I asked for their direct number so that if they didn't get in touch with us, I could call them directly. This is where that journal came in handy. In it, I'd started a list of people, job titles, and contact numbers.

I then called the rehab hospital to find out if they'd received approval from Public Health regarding lifting the ban on new admissions because of the flu outbreak. Unfortunately, I was told that the ban would continue until at least Tuesday, and that as the outbreak continued, the list of patients waiting in hospital for admission was growing. Alarm bells went off in my head.

"I want confirmation that Dominic won't lose his spot in the queue," I said.

The woman validated my concern but guaranteed nothing. Great. I explained again that Paul and I wanted Dominic to be considered for another unit OR to begin as a day patient as soon as possible. I said I was willing to drive across two cities daily if it meant access to rehab.

After hanging up, I picked up the phone again and called the hospital's transition coordinator, who worked on admissions and discharges. I reiterated the message to her. If they couldn't give me a solution, I'd help create one that could work. When it came to Dominic, I cared less about being liked and more about being helpful, practical, and solution oriented. My childhood fear of what others thought of me suddenly had less power.

Then I called the nurse practitioner at SickKids and asked if there was any way for her to support our request to go to another unit or start as a day patient to ensure Dominic got the care he needed. I even offered to start at the local rehab facility, which had far fewer resources, just to get the ball rolling.

I also started to research private therapy companies. Paul and I needed to learn how to help Dominic beyond passive range-of-motion exercises. We also wanted an OT to monitor Dominic's eating and drinking in hopes that he'd return to bottle-feeding at some point. Nursing him seemed like a pipe dream now but getting that NG tube out was something that could happen. Dominic hated it and the tape that held it to his face.

By the end of the first day, no nurse from the LHIN had called or visited to check on the NG tube. I called the LHIN again, as well as the company they contracted out, and voiced my concerns. The feeds had been going well that day, but my husband and I were disappointed in the system. Less than twenty-four hours in and we already had a gap in care.

Saturday morning, we finally received a call from the supervisor of the nursing staff in the community. She apologized and stated that they hadn't received the referral until late Friday night—she didn't know why—and that they hadn't had anyone to deploy to our home at that time. She confirmed that someone would visit the house later that day but that he began his shift at 3:00 p.m. I expressed understanding and said that would be fine.

That morning, Lorren had her first major meltdown with me since the stroke. She didn't want to go to her dance class. She cried, screamed, pulled my hair, and tried to hit me. Thankfully Paul was there to mediate and help me stay calm. I knew Lorren had been through a lot, but I'd never seen a tantrum like this before. I felt out of touch with my child and unable to manage the outburst. We allowed her to skip the class—she deserved a pass for our first Saturday home. It wasn't a battle I was willing to fight. Plus, I was having my own meltdown around my frustrations with the healthcare system.

My in-laws came over for breakfast and got an earful. I lost it. "I feel like I'm a capable individual, and even I'm anxious about managing

Dominic's care needs with zero supervision or support in the community!"
I was getting the runaround from the rehab hospital and was fearful that
the acute-care hospital had washed their hands of Dominic now that
he was discharged. And I was prepared to fight as hard as necessary in
order to make sure Dominic had appropriate care.

Then something dawned on me. What about the thousands of parents
who didn't know that they could advocate for their children and request
alternatives? What about the parents who didn't know what their child
was entitled to or what services were available? What if they didn't know
whom to talk to about what they needed? Were they just sitting at home,
with their innocent children, waiting for someone to help them? The
thoughts were infuriating—and still are.

Later that day, I prepared an email to send to the staff at SickKids
and anyone at Bloorview who might be able to help with our request
for Dominic to start rehabilitation. Along with our request, it expressed
our disappointment in the gaps in care and communication during this
process. I kept it in my drafts, ready to go if we found out on Monday
that the ban would last even longer. I was as careful as possible with the
wording, not wanting to come across as harsh. I know all too well the
label of "difficult" and what it does. I wanted to be short, sweet, and to
the point.

Sure enough, that Monday we found out that the ban would last for
several more days. But as a result of my relentless (yet friendly) calls to
the rehabilitation and acute-care hospitals and to community care, we
were able to get an OT into the house on Monday, a pediatric nurse to do
an overall assessment on Tuesday, and a visiting nurse that first Sunday

and again on Wednesday, along with a rehabilitation appointment with the inpatient team at SickKids, who went above and beyond to honor this request—major thanks to these amazing people. We also received the green light to start rehabilitation in the day-patient program the following week, after the long weekend.

February 20 was the official start date at Holland Bloorview Kids Rehabilitation Hospital. Although I had to drive Dominic in every day and wondered what this would do to his sleep habits and my patience, Paul and I were relieved to have a plan in place and minimal waiting.

Paul and I had several conversations about our expectations and fears. What if Dominic didn't regain functioning on his left side? What if he had a significant speech impediment due to left-sided facial paralysis? I told Paul that I needed to remind myself that a few months in rehab wasn't going to cure him. I had this vision of Dominic going to rehab and returning home as he was prestroke. I knew this wasn't realistic or fair to Dominic (or the rest of us), but it was difficult to understand the reality of this situation, even at this point.

Still, I put a lot of weight on the rehabilitation. I'd read about the importance of time in the case of young brains and their plasticity, and I didn't want to waste one precious moment. Time was of the essence. I allowed this sense of urgency to push me forward, and although I had to work through the unrealistic expectations, I was so grateful our little man was going to start the next chapter of this journey.

We would be there to support him every step of the way.

SIX

Rehabilitation

We arrived at Bloorview just before 9:00 a.m. on Tuesday, February 20, 2018. Lorren stayed home with my parents. We'd been telling her that Paul and I would have to leave to go to a new hospital for exercises but that we'd be home for dinner. Paul and I also prepared Lorren by explaining that soon, Dominic and I would be living at the hospital during the week. Communicating ahead of time has its advantages. This transition ended up seeming easier for Lorren, and for that I was grateful.

Paul had taken the day off work so that he could be there for the intake and assessment process. We'd be meeting the team that would work with Dominic daily for the several weeks.

The small day-program area consisted of a receiving room, a medical examination room, an office for the ambulatory nurses, and a resting room. Soon after we arrived, Dominic was lying on the examination table looking at us and playing with a toy we dangled above him. All of a sudden, he tried to roll over—and after a few attempts, he went from his stomach to his back. The look on his face was a mixture of pride and shock. I got it on camera and still watch it occasionally. It was the first time he'd accomplished something himself since the stroke, and he looked genuinely surprised. We shared the exciting news with the developmental pediatrician when he came in to do the assessment, and we all felt that this was a good start to his rehab journey.

After the assessment, Dominic met with the physiotherapist (PT), the speech-language pathologist (SLP), and the OT. Despite each professional having a different style, Dominic seemed to like all of them and engaged with them right away. By this point he'd been cleared to drink from a newborn bottle (NO MORE NG TUBE!) but couldn't sit up on his own for a long period, couldn't move his left arm with purpose, and couldn't move his left fingers. His left leg rarely moved and required stimulation (scratching or tickling) to incite a reaction from him. The therapists were patient and kind and told us this was just the beginning.

That day we also met briefly with the social worker to learn the ins and outs of rehab. It was decided that every day Dominic would engage with the OT and the PT, and a couple of times per week he'd meet with the SLP. During therapeutic recreation, Dominic would have an opportunity to practice what he'd learned in therapy and get time out of his room. He'd also be allowed to use the therapeutic pool once he was cleared by the doctor. This would help him get used to different sensations. Paul and I were to see the social worker weekly to talk about emotional issues as well as resource counseling in the community. As adept as I was at my job and as much as I knew about the resources in the community for school-aged children with mental-health concerns, I knew nothing about infant strokes and the supports required to give Dominic the best chance to reach his full potential. I put high expectations on the social worker but vowed to be understanding and nice as a client.

And so began the daily commute along the dreaded Highway 401. It took about an hour and a half to two hours to get there each morning, but the staff were kind enough to schedule Dominic's day so we could leave by 2:00 p.m. and avoid rush-hour traffic going home. We did this for two weeks. Every morning I'd hope that Dominic would nap in the car, and every morning, he didn't. He often fell asleep when we were five to ten minutes away from the hospital.

I worried that he wasn't napping enough, since he didn't sleep well at Bloorview in the little resting room. I was lucky if he slept for thirty minutes. All the research I'd found on brain-injury recovery and rehabilitation stressed the importance of sleep. But I tried not to worry too much. He was sleeping well overnight for the most part, and on days when he finished sessions by 1:00 p.m., he'd be home in time for his afternoon nap. I tried to go with the flow, to find the delicate balance between the healing power of sleep and the importance of early-intervention rehabilitation, but it was hard to do. In the end, though, we trusted that Dominic was getting what he needed and allowed him to take the lead.

We made his home life as typical as we could as we waited for admission and stayed as positive and upbeat as possible about his rehab. He was alive. And he'd already made gains eating orally and sitting up for a few seconds at a time. He was rolling over at times, one way, and we saw flickers of movement on his affected side. Things looked promising, and I clung to the hope that this would continue. Each day I'd ask the staff if the ban had been lifted, and each day the answer was the same: not yet.

BUILDING BONDS

Two weeks after we started day treatment, the outbreak was declared over and we were admitted to inpatient rehab. We were told this stay would be six to eight weeks. Since we were admitted on a Friday afternoon, we saw the room, looked around, and immediately went home for the weekend. We returned to the rehab hospital on Sunday night for our first inpatient week. Paul and Lorren dropped Dominic and me off, and once we were settled, it was time for them to head home to bed. I kept a smile on my face. "See you soon!" I said, waving. "Have fun with Nonno and Nonna this week!"

It isn't so bad, I told myself. *It could be worse.* I wanted to be strong not just for the kids but also for me. This would be the second period of separation from half of my family, and I knew it would be difficult to be away from them, but this time it felt different. We'd known this was coming, and it was temporary. When they were out of sight, I turned to Dominic and said, "Looks like it's just you and me, kid," and he smiled.

Most nights in the rehab hospital, Dominic was asleep by 7:00 p.m. I'd sit in the dark watching TV with headphones on. Paul and I had been told not to disrupt his sleep schedule or try to change it, as this could trigger seizure activity. Just as I'd done at SickKids, whenever Dominic would go down for a nap, I'd put a sign on the door signaling that a baby was sleeping. It didn't always stop people from coming in, which was annoying, but it helped. Most nights I'd try to get comfortable on the chair that turned into a cot. It was hard as rock and narrower than a single bed, but it sure beat sleeping sitting up in the ICU.

I couldn't sleep much there anyway. Every night, every hour, a nurse would come in to check on Dominic as part of their rounds. And each and every time that door opened, I'd wake up. For the first few weeks I'd shoot up in a panic to see who was coming in. Every time, the nurse would whisper, "Sorry." After a while, I got used to the visits and would just sit up and give a thumbs-up. One nurse would often say to me in the morning, "Do you ever sleep? Every time I come in to check on Dominic, you're awake. Then you're up so early with him every morning. I feel so bad."

I'd always been a light sleeper, and here, I could hear the low chatter of the nurses in the hallways, the beeps of machinery in the neighboring rooms, and the sounds of patients in the adjoining spaces. Deep sleep just wasn't in the cards. It didn't help that Dominic decided to wake up between five and six every morning.

We quickly developed a little routine: wake up, get dressed, and head to the family room to get this mama some coffee. There was a kettle in the communal kitchenette, and I'd bought some instant coffee from the nearby grocery store. It was gross but was the only option as the cafeteria didn't open until 7:00 a.m. Within a few days we met another mom and her toddler in the family room. The boy had been in an accident at their home and sustained a head injury. Very cute, he walked around with a stuffed monkey named Ooh Ooh. I started to chat with this mom, who was all too familiar with parenting an early riser. Dominic and I would see them every morning, bright and early. It was comforting not to be alone.

The kids in the Brain Injury Rehab Team unit were there for a variety of reasons, including accidents, neurosurgery, stroke, brain cancer, severe epilepsy, moyamoya, and more. We met children who'd had strokes during surgery to remove tumors. The trauma all these families had been through was terrifying and being there really put life into perspective. We were from all over the province, and we all had different stories bringing us together. I'd never felt so understood by people who didn't know me. Some friendships made in this place last a lifetime. I never would have developed certain friendships had this experience never happened. My friendship with Cori-Anne is one of them.

Cori-Anne, an extroverted, positive ray of light, is the mother of a beautiful little girl who lives with Down syndrome and moyamoya—a neurological disorder that causes strokes and seizures. That diagnosis and subsequent brain surgery led them to acute care and then the rehabilitation hospital. When I met her, Cori seemed way stronger and more astute than I was. She'd been navigating the healthcare system since her daughter was born, and she'd experienced so much trauma, having lost her second child just hours after the birth and being in and out of medical appointments and hospitals with her first. She and her partner had a third daughter, who was the spitting image of her mother—sassy, fun, and adorable. They were so fun to be around. Whenever she saw us walking down the hall, Cori's daughter would sing, "Dominic, Dominic, Dominic!"

We became friends quickly. Accepting her invitation, I started to leave our bedroom a couple of nights a week to chat with her and other moms (and a few dads) in the family room. Slowly, more moms joined, and I met another mother of a survivor of a stroke with no known cause. We all did our best to be positive and upbeat, but we all had challenges. Before long, we'd formed an informal support group.

A lot of these parents were honest and straightforward. They didn't mess around. There wasn't a lot of sugarcoating. If they thought something, they said it. If they disagreed with each other, they weren't afraid to share that. It was refreshing and gave me the courage to start speaking up more than I ever had. I realized it was time to truly practice advocacy.

A few of us started a Facebook group to keep in touch. In addition to the late-night talks in the family room, we had daily conversations online about tips and tricks regarding advocating for our kids. Those with more experience in the healthcare field, particularly as parents, took the lead, but we all chimed in. Support on top of support. No BS, total honesty. They understood what it felt like, entering the overwhelming waters and not knowing in what direction the tide would move. Being around these parents was enlightening and inspiring. I felt my own strength increase. I'm now a better advocate for my child and my clients because of these parents and caregivers.

Based on Cori's encouragement, I was able to ask for a therapy extension for Dominic to avoid wait times between inpatient and outpatient rehab. Our local outpatient children's center, ErinoakKids, wouldn't be able to start Dominic's therapy for over a week after his discharge from Bloorview due to capacity (and he was considered urgent). We were able to prolong our discharge by one day and then do three days of day-patient therapy the following week, to bridge the gap. Paul and I were so grateful for this, and I don't know if I would have asked as many times as I did if it weren't for all the words of encouragement and stories of strength.

In turn, I was compelled to help wherever I could. So many of these women had stories of obstacles and oppression. Many of them didn't have an advocate for issues such as housing, social assistance, childcare, etc. At first, I listened with an empathetic ear, and then I started to get angry. I remembered this feeling—it was the "fired up" feeling I'd get when I was working. After hearing a couple of stories in particular, I just couldn't stay idle.

I'd started to see a gap: There were parents who knew the system, weren't afraid to speak up, and advocated for what they needed. And there was a larger group still trying to keep their heads above water, feeling overwhelmed and terrified, not knowing where to turn, what questions to ask, and what care to request. This reminded me of clients. The fire in my belly grew.

During Dominic's last day at Bloorview, I spent a few hours connecting with a local Legal Aid office in a mother's hometown, attempting to get them representation. They weren't aware they could talk to the social worker about this. I told them they could spend their therapy sessions doing this kind of work with the social worker, but that they had to speak up. The therapist wouldn't know these issues existed if they didn't talk about them. Some of these women didn't know the power of their voice. It felt good to help them in some small way.

ANOTHER HOMECOMING

When we started the rehabilitation portion of Dominic's journey, Paul and I continued feeling so grateful for the work of the hospitals throughout this process. SickKids had saved Dominic's life and gotten him medically stable, and Bloorview was helping him jump-start his progress on the road to recovery. We felt so lucky to live near Toronto and have access to these world-renowned hospitals. We weren't naive to the fact that had we been in another part of the world or even another part of the country, Dominic's story could have had a very different, very tragic outcome.

Wanting to do something to give back, we decided that for Dominic's first birthday, we'd have a huge party and ask our friends and family to make donations to either hospital in Dominic's name, in lieu of gifts.

As I prepared to return to "real life" with Dominic after three months of inpatient rehabilitation, I couldn't help but feel a strong wave of mixed emotions. On one hand, I was excited to return to my house, my daughter, my husband, and the comforts of home. I dreamed of our new normal, a good night's sleep in my bed, cooking and eating my own food, showering in my bathroom, and going for walks around the block with the kids. On the other hand, I felt as if I were leaving a new surrogate family. I'd grown close with several of these resilient, super-strength moms (and dads). They'd been my sources of inspiration, confidants, and therapists. No matter how different we were from each other, how far apart we lived, what our professional or personal lives looked like, we had a solidarity unlike any I'd ever experienced.

The day of Dominic's discharge, Paul left work early to pick us up. I'd
been packing our items slowly throughout the week, and that Friday,
May 11, it was time to say goodbye to our friends and our temporary
home. Some of the nurses came by to take pictures with Dominic, tell
us how wonderful it had been working with us, and how confident they
felt that Dominic would make a solid recovery in the community, even
without daily therapies. I looked around the room, at my tiny little bed,
and thought, "Why would I ever miss this?" But the truth is, I would.
It was safe. It was safe knowing that if something went sideways with
Dominic, there were healthcare professionals twenty feet away at any
given moment. If he had any symptoms, new or recurring, they could be
dealt with immediately. If I felt anxious and nervous, someone was there
to calm me down with a gentle, compassionate, and validating demeanor.
In a weird way it really had started to feel like home.

When Paul arrived, I felt excited to see him coming down that hallway
into our room for the last time. He packed up the van and we slowly but
surely made our way out, saying goodbyes along the way—to parents, to
nurses, and even to the workers in the Tim Hortons in the cafeteria with
whom Dominic loved to flirt. Everyone was encouraging and shared in
our joy, but I couldn't help but feel a little sad and scared.

In typical Iannetta-Nunes fashion, Paul and I had planned to resod
half of our backyard the moment we arrived home from the hospital.
Our daughter's third birthday was in two weeks, and we wanted to have
a backyard BBQ party. I'd also figured that hard labor would be a nice
distraction from my reality and complicated emotional state. Movement
is medicine, after all.

There we were, with ninety-three rolls of sod, carving out a new land-scape in our backyard. We got home at 2:30 p.m. and finished the yard around 9:00 p.m., taking breaks for dinner and to put the children to bed. My mom was there to watch them in the interim. It felt really good to be able to do something at my home that I'd be able to enjoy in the coming months. It also distracted me from all the emotions of leaving hospital life after over four months.

SEVEN

The Aftermath

JEN + PAUL

The concept of romantic soulmates seems a bit far-fetched to me. I've always believed in kindred spirits, or souls who've known each other throughout past lives, but not that they need to be romantically involved.

I did, however, grow up watching romantic comedies in which the quirky girl finds her true love in a gorgeous jokester or the cool kid. I used to dream of one day being in that kind of love. Of finding someone I cared about that much, who accepted me for who I was. As I got older, I began to feel that real life wasn't quite like that. I was never the "sought after" girl in high school. My role was that of the best friend or the matchmaker. I lacked self-confidence, and certainly minimized any compliments I did get. Looking back, I know I'm guilty of "friend zoning" one or two lovely boys, though they have remained great friends.

By the time I'd finished my first undergrad degree, I was beginning to feel uninterested in dating. My radar seemed totally off. In fact, I'd briefly dated a man the year before who "ghosted" me after a few dates (before ghosting was a thing—so kudos to that guy for being ahead of his time!), and I later found out he was gay.

I decided to focus on a much more important relationship than a romantic one: the one with myself. I chose to work on how I saw myself. I focused on feeling strong, on exercising, and on being around friends who inspired me to be the best version of myself: Ashley, the fun-loving free spirit who was unapologetically herself and taught me it was okay to say no or have an opinion that differed from others'; Nikita, who loved everyone, was kindhearted and the most creative person I'd ever met (her events were Insta-drool-worthy before Instagram was a thing), and taught me it was okay to say "I love you"; Navi, who was strong, resilient, and fierce as hell, as well as caring and compassionate; and Jen, the most loyal and devoted friend I'd ever known and who owned her authenticity in such a beautiful way. These were my people. They still are. They inspire me to this day. I know part of the reason I am who I am is because I get to spend time around them. What I lacked in the romance department, I sure made up for with friends.

I planned to work after graduation and save for a condo or move abroad to do a master's degree and teach English. For the first time, I truly felt comfortable in my own skin. I felt a subtle confidence because I'd begun appreciating my strengths and accepting myself as I was, rather than focusing on what I wished to change.

A month after graduation, I was reintroduced to Paul through a mutual friend at a cottage weekend away. We'd met briefly a year earlier, at a friend's birthday party. We spent the bulk of the weekend together, staying up far later than our friends—one night, we stayed up until the morning talking about our goals (mine, mostly), our dreams, and our families. Paul wasn't a planner. Meanwhile, I had a detailed five- to seven-year plan. Paul lit up when speaking about his stepdad. He admired him so much, had learned a lot from him. He also spoke so respectfully about his mother's strength and ability to overcome challenges. He had so much love for his siblings and his niece. He was excited to be an uncle again that fall. I loved that he was family oriented and respectful. At first, he was quiet and charismatic. As I listened to him speak, I noticed a faint tingling in my gut. Something I'd never experienced before.

By the end of that summer, Paul and I were spending a lot of time together. We'd text each other throughout the workday and he'd call me on his way home from work daily. Conversation seemed effortless, and I enjoyed talking to him. Paul started to reveal his quick wit and one-liners. Once the jokes between us started, they didn't stop. It was a Euro Cup summer, and we teased each other about our respective teams (mine, Italy, his, Portugal). He was generally a quiet guy in group settings but in private could keep up with me—and that's saying a lot! When he spoke about something of interest, his voice would rise slightly, and his eyes would widen. He was passionate and sensitive. He was pensive, always observing. By the end of that summer, we finally admitted to ourselves that we were a couple, and no one around us was surprised. We were married five years later, in November 2013.

Paul and I have quite opposite personalities. I'm bubbly, loud, talkative, inquisitive, anxious. He's quiet, observant, and laid-back. Our relationship seems to work well because our personalities are different, but our work ethic, morals, and values are similar. Paul is a hard worker and puts in incredible effort whenever he takes on a task. As a recovering perfection-ist, I appreciate and understand the high expectations he sets for himself. He calms me down, and I light a fire up his backside when it's needed. Over the past decade and a half (I'm dating myself here)—we've rubbed off on each other, each taking on a few positive qualities of the other. He truly is the yin to my yang. I don't know if I believe we're soulmates (maybe that's reserved for the ladies I mentioned), but I surely believe that we take our decision to be together seriously. We choose to love each other and accept ourselves and each other with our differences. One thing I didn't know about us before this journey was how different we were when it comes to coping. Fairly soon after Dominic's stroke, I saw the stark contrast.

Paul was more emotional, had difficulty finding words and asking questions, and seemed to get overwhelmed by all the medical jargon being thrown around. He cried a lot more than I did in those first days after Dominic's diagnosis.

One afternoon in the ICU, I went for my scheduled pumping session in the designated breast-pumping room. The room was a light beige—the whole place seemed to be light beige—and it was quiet compared to all the other spaces. I sometimes wondered if I could fall asleep in here. No beeps, no oxygen pumps. Just a little box with a door, a chair, and a breast pump. I tried to get as comfortable as possible, which was hard. I was always nervous someone was going to walk in on me. It was bad enough that pumping always caused a bit of pain and discomfort—it didn't help to think that a stranger could walk in while I was "milking" myself.

On this day, I heard footsteps rush toward the door and immediately stiffened. Paul knocked and announced himself. My heart rate rose. Was something wrong? Had Dominic's status suddenly changed? I shut off the pump and opened the door.

"Come back to the room, quick!" Paul's voice was uncharacteristically shrill, his eyes were wide, and his posture was stiff. He'd run seventy-five meters to get me. I was ready to jump into crisis mode, waiting for horrible news, when he said that the doctors were doing rounds and he didn't think he could see them on his own—he was afraid he'd forget to ask questions or take down necessary information. Totally out of his element, he needed the support. He leaned on my over-the-top organization skills and my work experience in the medical system those first few days.

I asked a lot of questions, read information, wrote things down, learned acronyms as soon as I heard them (by asking what they were or looking them up), and couldn't cry many tears of sadness and fear—only tears of relief and joy. I took the reins when it came to logistical planning. I decided I would stay at the hospital overnight. He was quick to agree that this would be best, although part of me wondered after the fact if he just hadn't wanted to argue. I spent several moments giving Paul pep talks that first week, often holding him in a bear hug and telling him it was okay to be sad and scared, as I was too. I also told him that we had to be strong and positive around Dominic, to give off positive energy and talk around him. Paul agreed but many times through his tears would say, "I just want my smiley baby boy back." Those words cut like a knife. I wanted that so badly, too.

The hospital social worker in the ICU was there to help with resource counseling, crisis support, and supportive counseling. In speaking with him, it became clear to us that our "crisis modes" looked very different. I recalled my own social work training and knew we needed to respect where we were in our processing. One of the cardinal rules of social work is to "begin where the client is." In this sense, I wanted to respect Paul's process. I didn't have to understand it. I didn't have to agree with it. I just needed to know he was safe and processing in a way that made sense for him. I told him I supported him and wanted to be there for him in any way that I could. I felt a need to protect him. This was his first time dealing with a medical crisis.

In those early days, Paul and I had the same dark, scary thoughts creeping into our minds. *What if Dominic dies? Would that be easier for him? What quality of life will he have going forward? Will he get through this? Will we?* But we didn't share these thoughts with each other for a very long time. Each of us thought we were protecting the other and ourselves from the shame of having them at all. In hindsight, sharing those dark vulnerabilities might have felt validating. If I'd known then what I know now, I would have acknowledged that the thoughts were real. But I also recognize that neither of us was ready to share, so it went the way it was meant to.

To this day I cannot imagine what it must have felt like for Paul to leave that bedside, not knowing what the next hour would bring. I cannot imagine driving away from the hospital and putting on a happy face for a two-and-a-half-year-old who was ready to sing and play and cuddle. I don't know if I could have done it. And Paul doesn't think he could have handled the constant buzzing of the hospital, the constant interruptions, the lack of privacy and homely comforts, etc. It amazes me how different our experiences of the exact same event were.

Since that time, Paul and I have acknowledged that we can see how easy it is for families/couples to fall apart after a medical crisis. Our focus was entirely on our children. We remained partners, but instead of being in a romantic relationship, we were managing a "situation," as if we were running a business. There was no romance, no cuddles, no time together. Time apart was spent coping in very different ways. I would write, he would use distraction (video games or TV). And when we were together, we were surviving and just trying to get through to the next hour. This can put a strain on a relationship in no time.

I was aware of how easy it could be to ignore each other and drift apart. I spoke up about this once we'd moved into the recovery phase of this experience. I told Paul how I felt and shared my desire to make even a small effort to stay connected: regular text messages, check-in calls, and date nights at home on weekends were things we added to our routine. We respected each other's need for alone time after a chaotic day/week of the grind but always made a point to connect with each other.

Three days after we came home from SickKids, we'd adjusted to managing Dominic's new care needs and Paul returned to work full time. At first, I was happy about this. I was on maternity leave, and we needed the income. I was at home and could do things my way on my own schedule for the first time in months. I got to reconnect with my daughter. I got to be with my children all day and watch them grow. I was lucky and I knew this.

Over time, his career flourished and progressed. I beamed with pride. I also started to feel resentful. I watched him get up, get himself ready while the house was quiet and dark, and leave. I didn't go anywhere. I couldn't remember the last time I'd brushed my hair. I wore the "mom uniform" every day (lycra pants and plain top). The same shirt stayed on my body for days at a time, until I managed a shower. I got up, prepped meds, meals, and therapeutic activities, changed diapers and entertained two little people all day, prepped more meals, cleaned, and repeated. No feedback. No "Good job, Jen."

Going to work would have felt like a break. Paul didn't watch each day pass wondering if his career would ever recover. He didn't think about lost wages, lost education opportunities, lost freedom. I had control over raising my children and managing my home, but at the cost of letting go of my career for an unknown period of time.

Paul got to talk to adults, he got validation, he got feedback that his work was valuable. If nothing else, he got a drive to and from work in SILENCE. Or better yet, blasting whatever song he wanted (not "Baby Shark" on repeat!). I missed working. I missed the people, the engagement, the focusing on something outside my home. Then I felt guilty for feeling this way. I was lucky to be able to be at home during this time. I'd chosen to have children and had known I'd be the main caregiver. I couldn't reconcile these conflicting feelings, and the resentment toward Paul started to fester and grow.

When Paul and I first started dating, I asked us to commit to one major thing in our relationship: honesty. If either of us didn't want to be in it anymore, we wouldn't drag it out to "spare the other's feelings."

We'd have the tough conversations whenever they were needed. And so one night, I sat on the couch and asked if we could talk. Whenever one of us said that, we knew it meant business.

I explained that I was so grateful that he was working, and that I was proud of him for all his hard work. And I told him that at the same time, I was resentful that he got to go and I didn't. My emotions were all over the place. I felt lost without work, tired from the demands at home, scared I'd never recover professionally, proud of him, happy to be at home for this period of time, content with being involved with the kids, and grief for not having anything outside of that. And of course guilt—that could have gone without saying. He listened, was gentle and kind, and provided me with his perspective. He felt that he was missing out on caregiving, that he was inadequate in comparison to my abilities, and that he had a heightened duty and pressure to provide financially for our family. We admitted that neither of us had understood the other's experience. We listened to and validated each other. We could both accept the circumstance and yearn for it to be different. Being open and accepting of each other's differences is vital to stay connected. Communication is key. We aren't mind readers.

One thing that Paul and I did was try to laugh as much as we could. For example, about two weeks after Dominic's stroke, after the date of our scheduled trip to Florida with my cousins and their children had passed, we were talking about how shitty it was to have had to cancel for the reason we did. Then my cousin sent me a text saying that due to weather, they'd been stuck on the plane with their kids for several hours for deicing, etc. (which, for the record, sounds awful with toddlers). I turned to Paul and said sarcastically, "Thank God we dodged that bullet!" It wasn't my finest comedic moment, but we both laughed (maybe more than we would have under normal circumstances). It helped us make light of what we were going through. Laughter connects people. It's medicinal.

This experience taught us so much about ourselves and each other. Sometimes it feels as if we've had many more years' worth of experiences together than we have. We've learned so much, the most crucial being the importance of forgiveness. We forgave each other for the resentment. We forgave each other for not understanding. We forgave each other for the mistakes. And we vowed to grow from each experience.

Even when we put our relationship on the back burner, we checked in and acknowledged that this was happening. We never stopped communicating. Sure, things ebbed and flowed; some days we talked for two minutes, others for an hour. It was important to find little ways to stay connected, such as ordering takeout and eating a meal after the kids were in bed or talking on the phone before going to sleep when we were apart (and regularly reminding ourselves that the time apart was temporary). I'm so grateful for Paul. Even on days when I'm annoyed and resentful. I'm so grateful for choosing to love this man for the rest of my days. I'm so grateful he chose me. I'm so grateful for our bond and connection.

In 2018, I was interviewed for an article in *Toronto Life* magazine about our journey, and I expressed my gratitude to have someone I could communicate with. I'm also so grateful to have a partner who's supportive. I feel that now more than ever. I'm more in love with Paul than I've ever been. He's a major reason many things in my life are possible.

PUTTING THE FEELINGS ON A SHELF

I was taught early on that there are very few things worth complaining about. Complaining isn't helpful, nor is it something others want to hear. Growing up, I broke multiple bones and needed to adapt. My mother left home for months of radiation therapy to treat aggressive breast cancer when I was thirteen. These things were challenging and upsetting but didn't stop us from moving forward and growing. Homework still had to get done, chores still needed to be completed, and life moved on, so we had to as well. I suspect I was born with this mindset, but my parents certainly exemplified it too.

And so, in the early days after Dominic's stroke, I didn't understand that strength and vulnerability could coexist. That someone could be strong and feel utterly shattered at the same time. I truly believed that if I cracked and started crying, I'd never stop. I'd never be able to get up again. If I verbalized the funeral plans I'd made in my mind, I'd be manifesting them into fruition. I didn't want to give weight or validity to the darkness when I felt so unstable. I had the old-school mindset that to cry over a situation and grieve for someone who was still alive was to indulge in self-pity, which served no purpose but to hold me back from fulfilling my duties as a mother. I denied majority of my feelings and carried on with my responsibilities, hoping one day these emotions would be a distant memory.

I was full of guilt, shame, and anguish. Avoiding these emotions and forcing them to the back of my mind to sit and fester was a form of punishment. I didn't feel that I deserved to release and process them or be supported by others. My job was to be the caregiver, not the care recipient. The opposite turned out to be true. This was a huge learning experience for me. Pushing things to the back of my mind wasn't coping—it was avoidance. As a temporary coping strategy at the height of the crisis, sure, it worked. In the long run, it was critical to go back and allow the externalization of emotions. To give myself permission to feel it all. The good, the bad, and the ugly. I eventually had to sit with those uncomfortable feelings to process them.

A part of me didn't feel safe releasing these emotions, and I didn't know how to process them. Doing so meant facing the guilt, fear, grief, shame, and sadness. I didn't think I could do it. I didn't believe that I was capable of managing the crisis and processing my emotions simultaneously. I convinced myself that if I wrote in my journal, went for walks, and practiced meditation, that all those yucky feelings would dissipate and I'd be healed. As if I could "social work" myself and bypass all the emotional work required for true healing. *Spoiler alert: not possible.* Coping tools are excellent to help decrease symptoms of anxiety, stress, and depression, but they don't address the root cause of the feeling. These feelings need to be expressed, accepted, and released.

The months of physical and emotional pain took me a long time to work through. And this experience led to an abrupt awakening personally and professionally.

I'm stronger now than I've ever been. I also weep more. I express more of every emotion. The reality is that I didn't know what I was made of until going through this. Of course, if I'd known then what I know now, I might have handled my emotions differently. But I wasn't ME then.

I was a younger version. I did the best I could with what I had. Being self-compassionate is so important. Learning to love myself as I am, flaws and all, has been a critical component of my healing. I have come to accept that things are the way they are. This is neither good nor bad. Sometimes bad things happen for no good reason. It's not the why that's important, but what I make of the struggle.

It is not wrong to think "it could always be worse," but this statement is never the full story. Things can truly suck, and we can use these challenges to help us learn, grow, and be better, even when we don't realize we're doing this. Struggle shapes who we are. We can work hard to make meaning in experiences, even terrible ones. It's not easy. It's not supposed to be. And that's the motivation behind telling my story. If my experience can help someone else out there feel less alone, less frightened, less incapable, then I'll shout it from the rooftops.

FIRST BIRTHDAY

Dominic turned one on a Monday. It was a quiet day at home. Paul and I had decided that we didn't want to make his birthday too stimulating or different from his every day, especially since we'd be having a big celebration that Saturday. We decided to go out to a restaurant as a foursome for the first time.

That morning, my mom came by to watch Lorren because Dominic had a developmental pediatrician appointment, and my dad came in the afternoon with a Timbit because he couldn't help wanting to see his grandson on his birthday. The appointment began at the same time as Dominic's first nap of the day. The pediatrician checked his social development, gross motor skills, and fine motor skills and compared his right side to his left. She tried to get him to hold a ball with his left hand (which he couldn't do) and asked if he was crawling or walking (which he wasn't). She said he was very social and made great eye contact.

Halfway through the appointment, Dominic was sitting on my lap half asleep. I stated that it was past his nap time, hoping that we could speed up the assessment, but the doctor seemed unfazed. Though bothered by the disregard for the importance of sleep at that age, especially post–brain injury, I understood that she had a job to do. At the end of the appointment, she told me that she thought Dominic was developing typically from a cognitive standpoint and was about six to eight months old in terms of his physical movement/gross and fine motor skills. When I told Paul this, he was as pleased as I was. He thought the stroke had acted like a "reset button"—it had been almost six months since the event. After the appointment I let Dominic sleep, and the day ended up being lovely and calm and exactly what we needed.

I'd started planning the Birthday Fundraiser Bash when we got to the neurology floor at SickKids. Those first few days had been so tumultuous and scary; Dominic's death had been a real possibility, and his recovery had been made possible by SickKids and Bloorview—Paul and I wanted to channel our gratitude into something helpful.

What had started off as an idea for a big party / sip and see for our child's milestone became a full-blown fundraiser. We had a giant rented tent in our backyard and shut down part of our street. A few of my friends offered to collect prizes that could be raffled off. That turned into more people volunteering gifts, and before I knew it, we had a face painter for the kids, mini massages for the adults from a registered massage therapist, police officers, bubbles, games, a 50/50 draw, a raffle with twenty-seven donated prizes, and LOTS of food (graciously donated by our local grocery store) and drinks. Almost two hundred people came, and between online donations and the party, we raised over twelve thousand dollars for Holland Bloorview Kids Rehabilitation Hospital and over two thousand four hundred for SickKids. Paul and I were blown away by the love and support. It was a physical example of the saying "It takes a village to raise a child." I was brought to tears looking around at our village.

As expected, Dominic was overwhelmed and overstimulated. He seemed tired and clingy and ended up spending most of the party in the house, where it was quiet. Occasionally Paul or I would pop out with him in our arms. What we didn't know at the time was that he was having seizures throughout the day from the stimulation and cognitive fatigue. Dominic's neurologist had just started weaning him off his antiseizure medication because he was doing so well. We didn't see any physical manifestations of seizures until shortly thereafter. I'll get to that soon.

THE POT BOILS OVER

The first month I was back at home for good, I couldn't fall asleep without Paul with me. Every time I got into my bed alone, I had visions of Dominic the day it all started. It didn't help that after about a week of solid sleeping through the night, Dominic started to wake up every couple of hours and wouldn't settle. Paul and I ended up caving and taking him into bed with us, where he'd immediately calm down. We figured it was because he was so accustomed to sleeping with me a few feet away, able to see me whenever he wanted, at the hospital.

But when he slept in our bed, I felt uneasy. What if I rolled over on him? What if he suffocated in my pillow? What if I woke up and he wasn't breathing? Moreover, Lorren was now sleeping in a "big girl" bed and getting up in the middle of the night. She'd put on her dress shoes, walk around her room, play with toys, turn on lights, and make noise. We once found her asleep leaned on her chair with one leg crossed over the other. It was adorable, but I also realized that all the transitions were taking their toll on us in different ways. We were all exhausted. Lorren started to have tantrums the likes of which I'd never seen. She was becoming more defiant with me. *Part of toddlerhood*, I thought. But a little voice inside my head kept reminding me, *Trauma processing takes time for everyone. Especially a three-year-old.*

I got so desperate that one day I went out and bought a king-size mattress and box set. I'm not sure what I was thinking. We certainly couldn't afford it at the time, and I knew that this wouldn't help the situation—would only make us more likely to let the kids sleep in our bed. But sleep deprivation makes people do things. Naturally, the day I purchased the mattress was the day Dominic began sleeping through the night. Murphy's Law, I guess!

About a week after Dominic and I returned from Bloorview, our cousin lost her baby, a little boy. She'd been just shy of twenty weeks pregnant.

My heart broke for her and her family. I sat at the dining room table and sobbed for half an hour when I heard the news. Paul also took it hard. We felt grief for our cousin and her family, and it felt like hearing about this profound loss was permission to grieve almost losing our own.

My birthday that year, 2018, about two months after his stroke, was an emotional one. I couldn't help but reflect on all the things that could have been and what had changed since that time. Thankfully, still being at Bloorview, I had the space to unpack and address these things with the social worker on staff there. Two months later, though, I was on my own, and throughout those first few months at home, I found myself triggered by stories of loss, whether I knew the affected person or not. My chest would get tight, and I'd have nightmares and flashbacks.

We attended a wake for a relative of Paul's friend that summer. Being there brought how close we'd come to losing Dominic to the surface, and I broke down in the parking lot as we left. *Things are starting to unravel*, I thought. In reality, things were starting to get put back together.

The analogy I use now is that of cleaning out a closet. When you remove everything from the closet and throw it on your bed, it looks like an absolute disaster zone. But the removal needs to be done in order to sort through what's staying and what needs to be let go. Once that's done, the closet gets put back together in a way that's much more organized, and it has more space. This was the beginning of me taking the clothes out of my emotional closet and tossing them on the bed.

I'd love to say that after Dominic's stroke I was optimistic with minor exceptions and able to express gratitude and love each day and in everything I did. I want to say I was a great example for my kids. But the truth is, it got hard. It got really hard. And I started to get very tired. Physically and emotionally.

Around the time of the six-month poststroke milestone, I could feel my optimism weakening. I was feeling more fatigued, more stressed out. Sleep was getting more difficult to sustain, and less helpful than usual when I did get it. I felt unequipped to manage the daily happenings of living with a toddler and a baby. I was uninspired and unproductive in the kitchen, often resorting to hodgepodge meals, more meat or processed food, and takeout. As someone who likes to cook, try new (mostly vegetarian) meals, and limits takeout to once per week, this was out of character. I just couldn't do it.

My mind felt cloudy and cluttered. I kept asking how this had happened. It still felt surreal. I kept thinking about the future, trying to predict what would happen and how it would unfold. (Control freak, remember?) When would he learn to walk? Would he regain hand function? How would he complete simple tasks, such as tying his shoes, doing up buttons, cutting his food, and so forth if he couldn't use his hand? How had we gotten here? What would we tell his sister when she started to ask questions about the differences in function between them? What would we tell him? The doctors kept saying it was a medical fluke, yet I couldn't stop blaming myself.

My guilt and shame pulled me into a dark thought pattern that continued to get stronger and stronger, bringing me further and further down. The guilt wormed its way into my head and heart and stayed there. Just before bed was the hardest. My bedtime routine had become a time to think about all the things I had to do the next day and all the things I hadn't done enough of or done well enough that day. It was toxic.

Within a few weeks of feeling this way, I threw out my back and was in more physical pain than I'd ever been. It happened while I was dancing with my daughter. I'd wanted her to feel special and have some fun time with Mommy. She asked me to pick her up, so I did. I swung her from one side to the other only to hear a small snap. The pain was sharp and went right down my left leg to my foot. I couldn't put weight on my left side for well over a week. I couldn't lift anything beyond a plate or bowl but couldn't stretch to reach them either. Of course, this also meant no lifting Dominic. I now needed someone at the house every waking moment to help me take care of the kids. This brought me to a new low. I wasn't able to do my part as a mom. I'd reached total failure status. Thoughts got darker and darker, faster and faster.

Physically and emotionally exhausted, I had very little patience for my daughter and her three-year-old tantrums and power struggles, which seemed to be constant—I'm certain we were feeding off each other at this point. I had little stamina and endurance with my son while doing his exercises. If he resisted or pushed me away or started to fuss, I'd stop and find something easier for him to do (i.e., tummy time instead of constraint-induced movement therapy). It took all the energy I had to engage with friends. I'd cancel plans or avoid connecting. I'd taken an extended leave of absence from my job as a school social worker and therefore felt that I had very little purpose outside of being a mother. And even that role was too much.

I realized later that there was a term for what I was doing. In her book *Rising Strong*, Brené Brown talks about the notion of putting emotional pains "on a shelf" to deal with later. She refers to it as "stockpiling hurt."4 I pushed down the hurt, sadness, worry, and fear over and over until my physical body decided enough was enough. I needed help. The human body is a pretty remarkable and wise thing.

One night, after a particularly challenging day, Paul got up to use the bathroom and left the door open. I was up, of course, and convinced myself that the light from the bathroom was what caused the kids to wake up. When he returned to the bedroom, I snapped at him about never remembering to close the door. I could actually see myself losing control of my life and grabbing at ANYTHING I might be able to grasp to regain it. It felt shitty to berate him, but I kept going. As I ranted on out loud, out of control, I thought, *Why am I getting upset with him about a light? I can't even let him go to the bathroom? How could he want to stay with someone so critical?*

Paul, being the calm, patient person he is, was rightfully annoyed and brushed me off to go back to sleep because he had to work in the morning. I, however, couldn't sleep after that. My heart was thumping and my mind was racing. I felt terrible and needed to figure out what was causing me to act this way. I could feel the lid of the boiling pot starting to quiver and shake. It was about to blow. Was this my anxiety? Was this depression? I felt so angry and so confused.

Thinking, stewing, boiling, I lay there in the dark, and half an hour later, I woke up Paul gently to apologize. I was barely able to choke out "I'm sorry" before the floodgates opened. I started to bawl, there in our bed, at 1:30 a.m. on a Wednesday.

Paul held me close and told me to let it out. His hug made me cry even harder. I tried to explain but couldn't bring to words what I was feeling. It made no logical sense for me to have been set off at that moment, but here I was. The lid was off and the water was spilling everywhere—figuratively and literally (I was crying a lot). Maybe I was finally processing everything we'd been through as a family in the last six months, or maybe I was finally allowing myself to express the immense fear and anguish I'd been stockpiling all that time. Maybe I was seeking forgiveness from Paul in that moment. But what I really needed, deep down, was to start forgiving myself. It was time to face up to and own my emotions.

I'm a person who loves schedules, consistency, and predictability, and I was now living in a reality with nothing but question marks. I had to adjust the parts of me that no longer fit within my reality. I had to accept that I had no control. I had to TRUST the process.

And I needed help to do this, and I felt I needed it quickly. I told Paul this. He agreed and was extremely supportive. I cannot thank him enough for his strength and gentle compassion toward me during this time. Although my reaction to him that night isn't something I'm proud of, I believe it was a necessary part of my journey to get to where I am now. To start the healing process. And I'm so grateful to have a partner who allows me to unravel and be a mess when I need it, without judging me.

I had to learn to do that for myself as well.

EIGHT

The Journey toward Healing, Take One

It took me three days after that boiling over to call the doctor. I procrastinated because I was doing the typical Jen thing and trying to figure it out on my own. I wanted to help myself before reaching out and asking others for help. *I'm the professional,* I thought. *I should know what to do to help myself. I help others all the time. I have all the tools I need to get better. I just have to do the work.*

But as most professionals in this area of work know, it's far easier to help others than to help yourself. The other obstacle I had to overcome was my logical optimism. I kept telling myself things would get better eventually—I just had to "hang in there." I was resisting the reality: that it's possible to know things will get better AND know that they're not good now. "Hanging in there" was a way of surviving. I didn't want to simply survive anymore. I wanted to live. I wanted to thrive. I wanted all of us to thrive.

The nurse practitioner at my doctor's office wasn't at all surprised when I requested a referral for a therapist, and she told me she was happy I'd reached out to her. "I've been waiting for you to ask," she said.

I got the number of a local therapist who specialized in trauma and called later that day to make an appointment. I also started seeing an osteopath and a physiotherapist for my back pain, and within a few weeks of simultaneous physical and psychological treatment, I started to feel better. I began to start jogging outside again after a two-year hiatus, even for just twenty minutes or a couple of kilometers at a time. It felt good to sweat. To spend time alone. To feel out of breath from something other than my thoughts. To use some of my adrenaline and tense energy in a constructive way.

As luck would have it, around this time I was contacted by a director of a private social work group looking to hire a part-time social worker to provide counseling to people who'd been in traumatic accidents. The director was aware of my situation—we'd spoken before Christmas about my working for the company. Following the stroke, I explained what had happened and hadn't been back in touch. She asked if I was ready to consider working, and I decided to take this as a sign and agreed to the interview.

If it doesn't seem like a good fit, I don't have to take it, I told myself. As it turned out, the role was very flexible and would allow me to generate some income and also be available for Dominic's appointments. As well, I'd be working closer to home than at my other job. I was offered the role a few days after the interview and agreed to start in the fall, only eight weeks later. I told myself that this meant it was time to start working on my own trauma, so that I could be mentally and emotionally ready to return to work—something I was fearful of doing but also really looking forward to.

THERAPY

I was ready for change. I was ready to start learning to live again. I wanted to be a better mother, partner, social worker, and overall human being. And during the first therapy session, a lightbulb turned on over my head. I learned more about trauma in one analogy than I ever had in multiple training sessions.

My therapist told me that a person is made up of many different puzzle pieces: likes, dislikes, personality attributes, strengths, etc. When trauma happens, it rocks us to our core. Those pieces get thrown up in the air like little pieces of crumpled paper, and each piece falls at a different pace. It can take days, weeks, months, or even years for all of them to fall, and when they do hit the ground, a messy pile of human is left on the floor. It takes a long time to put those pieces back together while finding space for new pieces that were created along the journey. The puzzle can be whole again, but the shape will change.

That's exactly how I felt. That validation was more helpful than anything else I'd discussed with therapists in past years. I was ready to do the work to put those pieces back together.

I began to rebuild my foundation and allowed myself to feel all the vulnerability, fear, and negative emotions that came along with doing so. I finally realized that I was angry with God, with myself, and with others. I'd been holding grudges without acknowledging them.

I created a mantra—a list of the things I thought were most important in creating a successful day:

I am a beacon of love and hope.
I kiss my husband every day and tell him I love him.
I dance with my children every day.
I laugh with my kids every day.
I spend a few minutes practicing mindfulness to release myself from my obsessive compulsivity.
I work hard with my clients.
I acknowledge feelings of guilt and replace them with gratitude.

This is an exercise I'd assigned to clients in the past but hadn't put into practice myself. I'd tried saying these things in my mind, but it hadn't been very effective. My therapist encouraged me to say them out loud. Doing this would stimulate multiple areas of the brain, including those involved in auditory and cognitive processing, allowing new neuropathways to be created. All things I knew but spent too much time ignoring because I helped *others*—I didn't need to practice what I preached (please note my sarcasm). Over time, thought patterns congruent with the words I was repeating would form. I was banking on neuroplasticity to help my son recover, and I was banking on the same for myself.

FAMILY VACATION

That summer, our family decided to try to enjoy what was left of the season. I asked my in-laws if we could spend a weekend up at their cottage together, just the six of us. It would be our first time there, and the longest we'd been away from home as a foursome. The kids were excited and so was I, although also nervous. We packed up everything we could think of and tried to plan it so the kids would fall asleep in the car and we could avoid rush-hour traffic. Rookie mistake. When we got there the kids were so excited they could hardly sleep, particularly our daughter. She was up until 2:00 a.m., to be exact. Note to self: don't arrive at a cottage with a lake view during night hours.

Lorren then woke up at 5:45 a.m., enthralled by the fact that she could see the lake from the windows. She loved being there, loved frolicking on the beach. Dominic also enjoyed being outside (on a blanket) and even let me take him into the lake for a little swim. He didn't love the water, but he laughed as I swung him around in it. Then he had an epic nap. As my older relatives would say, "Fresh air always helps babies sleep better."

After the second night, we'd all gotten back on track with our sleep. Our in-laws were scheduled to arrive later that day. That morning, though, Dominic didn't seem himself. He appeared more tired than usual even though he'd slept through the night (in the same room as us so we could keep a close eye on him). Throughout the day, he had these little episodes where his affected arm would cramp. We'd seen this before, but he'd also bend over and make a small moaning sound. At other times he seemed dazed and wouldn't make eye contact when spoken to.

These episodes lasted about twenty to forty-five seconds, and when they were over, Dominic would be either tired or clingy and would hug us tightly with his right arm. After he was consoled, he'd continue playing. This happened three times before his first nap. Paul and I were very concerned. He slept for over two hours and seemed better when he woke up, but unfortunately, shortly after his nap, he had another episode.

I called our contact at SickKids and was told they'd need to see a video of what Dominic was doing in order to be able to assess him. I wrote a detailed description of what we were seeing and sent the requested video. I also commented on the clinginess and crying afterwards. The nurse practitioner on the team said my description was cause enough for concern—it could be seizure activity. The neurology team advised us to take him to the emergency department to have him checked out. Given the frequency with which he was having the episodes, they felt he should be started on meds.

We knew seizures were a possibility poststroke. They're a common side effect of stroke in infants. And Dominic had been weaned off the antiseizure medication he'd started taking after his initial diagnosis of poststroke epilepsy a month ago.

We called our in-laws, who were on their way, to tell them what was going on, then packed up our belongings, said hello and goodbye to my in-laws as they arrived, and headed back to Toronto. Paul dropped

Dominic and me off at the emergency room before taking Lorren home. We both choked back tears as we said goodbye. It almost felt as if we were starting the traumatic experience all over again. I reminded myself how different it was this time around. I knew it wasn't the same. But walking into the building and hearing Lorren cry because she couldn't come with us felt all too familiar and terrifying.

We were admitted quickly, and Dominic had another small episode in front of the neurology resident. He was started on a new medication (Keppra), and we were transferred back to the neurology unit. I knew that Dominic was in good hands and that seizures were a small problem compared to the massive stroke he'd already endured. The positive self-talk that I'd been practicing, combined with my knowledge of what was happening, gave me a different perspective from the start. I was able to stay out of the major crisis-response, or shock zone I'd been in the last time I walked through those doors. I was beginning to get accustomed to not having control over my son's health. I trusted the team and my ability to advocate when necessary. Being back in Unit 5C (neurotrauma-epilepsy-neurosurgery) felt familiar—almost comfortable.

Once Dominic started on the Keppra, the episodes stopped almost instantly. Lorren and Paul joined us at the hospital the next morning after breakfast, and the four of us spent the day hanging out in Dominic's room and walking around the hospital and outside. It wasn't the family vacation we'd hoped for, but the four of us were together. We found tiny joys in going to the playroom, walking outside among the huge skyscrapers, and having treats throughout the day. I was grateful for several things that weekend, despite the scary parts.

Thankfully, Dominic didn't have any episodes the next day, and we were sent home late that afternoon. Before leaving the hospital, I arranged for pickup of his medication the next day and requested a few doses, as it took time to make this compound. I was starting to get the hang of advocacy. When we got home the routine quickly returned to what we considered our new normal. But I was exhausted.

FACING THE TRAUMA

During a therapy session the following week, I shared my confusion. "I don't know why, but I'm feeling exhausted. I'm sleeping enough, I'm going for short runs a few times a week, I'm eating decently. I feel good otherwise."

My therapist responded bluntly. "It's trauma. That's why you're tired."

He was right. It was the trauma, rearing its ugly head again. It creeps in when you least expect it. It was time for acceptance: I wasn't going to be "cured" after five sessions of therapy. This marathon was the real deal. I'd have to run or walk it, but either way, it was happening. Whether I felt prepared or not. Resistance would be futile. It felt scary to realize I had so little control over my trajectory along this journey. I'd always felt that if I stayed positive and focused on my health, I'd be okay. That's the thing with mental health—you can't treat it like a throat infection. You can't fix it with seven days of antibiotics. The event doesn't go away. Coping skills improve and symptoms are managed and minimized over time. The brain processes the event when it's ready and then we're left with the facts of it, hopefully without the intense emotions.

Shock and denial are typical responses immediately following a traumatic event. Going through the motions, I'd take care of logistical details but wouldn't access the emotions or process what the hell was happening. My focus was on my child, as is the case with so many caregivers. Once the shock of what had happened started to wear off, months after the event, all the chronic symptoms showed themselves: flashbacks, tense relationships, exhaustion, headaches, nausea, pain, etc. CHECK, CHECK, CHECK. I had them all. Most of the parents I'd met along the way in the hospitals described exactly the same feelings. It was like a traumatized-parent checklist.

In my work with parents and caregivers, it's my job to help them identify and validate their experiences. I use the word *trauma* when it's warranted, but a lot of the time, caregivers and parents (including me) minimize their experiences. "It's nothing compared to x, y, z." Trauma and healing aren't a competition, though. One person's experience isn't more or less valid than someone else's. It's subjective. Parents who have gone through trauma need to learn to accept that their experience is valid. Dr. Gabor Maté often says that trauma isn't the event of something happening, but rather, what happens in your body as a result of that event.5

That said, the word doesn't need to hold as much power as society gives it. *Trauma* sounds scary. Damaging and permanent. It's true that we cannot change a traumatic event after it has happened. But the wound, what happens inside of us, the *real trauma*, can be healed. We might never be the same as we once were, but maybe that's a beautiful thing. We're changing and growing all the time, with or without traumatic experiences. Trauma induces a hell of a lot of stress and fear, but my God is it ever a catalyst for growth and change.

It's not just one person in a family system who feels the effects of a traumatic event. Each person has their own experience of what happened. Each person has a different coping style. And each person heals at their own pace. Experience is subjective. Each is relative and valid. While we were in the PICU, a high school friend posted on social media about the "nightmare" of being in hospital with his child, who'd contracted influenza. They were in the hospital for two days. Paul showed me the post and said, "I wish this were the flu." Sure, but in our prestroke world, that would have been a nightmare. Before this, our nightmare was a buckle fracture our daughter sustained from being pushed off a slide. It's all relative. So is strength. So is the ability to heal.

It's so important to go into the dark. To go into those emotions that scare the hell out of us. When the memories surface, see what thoughts and emotions come up so that they can be validated and processed. Just do it with support. Do it safely. Do it knowing that no matter how scared or sad you feel, it's not forever. It's a feeling. Change is constant.

People have told me that I'm strong, and that I'm a good parent. I LOVE the words of affirmation (it's my love language). It has brought tears to my eyes to hear people say such kind things. When I'm exhausted, feeling less than, feeling inept in my abilities as a mother, a comment like this reminds me that I need to step back from the moment and see the big picture. I need to recognize I am my own harshest critic, as most of us are. It's hard when we're in the thick of it. When we live in the day to day, we can get tunnel vision. It's difficult to see outside ourselves.

I was dealt a hand of cards different from most, and I played it in the best way that I knew how. When people tell me, "I don't know how you do it," I usually respond with, "We just do." It's true. No matter the hardship, we can heal, we can grow, and we can learn.

What if instead of seeing trauma as simply a wound, we regarded it as a wound AND a badge of honor? It's an opportunity to learn what it's like to face-plant along the path of life, and to learn to stand up again and keep going, even if you end up going in a new direction. If you're in the middle of that journey now and feel as if you're facedown on the ground, unable to stand, I see you. Please know, you CAN get up again. You don't have to do it quickly; it doesn't have to be pretty. Growth is growth. Progress is progress. There's no one way to do it. It isn't linear. Life isn't sometimes. We just have to choose to continue. We have the power to create beauty around us.

I'll never look back on this time in my family's life with warm fuzzies and think solely happy thoughts. The experience rocked us to our core. It has also allowed us to grow independently and together—to rise, and to learn who we are and what we're capable of.

It has forced me to let go of the need to control (for the most part—old habits die hard, you know). It has allowed me to deepen my understanding of myself. To create a new level of authenticity. To work with more integrity. To realize that acceptance doesn't mean liking something. To recognize I am in control of ONLY myself (and even this level of control can be difficult when emotions run wild). I'm a better mother now, a better therapist, and probably a better human being. I'm learning what self-compassion is. I'm learning how important it is to take care of myself so that I can take care of others. That process starts with acknowledging and validating the trauma and pain, and this leads to forgiveness and grace.

CHRISTMAS

That fall was full of good things. Lorren started preschool. I started my new part-time job, working a few hours a day. Dominic got a stamp of approval from the neurology team at his follow-up in September. And a few weeks before Christmas, my best friend, Ashley, came home to visit.

We've been best friends since we were fourteen. The year Lorren was born, Ashley moved to the Middle East for adventure and career advancement. She returns to Canada once or twice a year, but I hadn't seen her since Christmas of the previous year. She hadn't seen Dominic since before the stroke. It seemed as though life was now measured this way: before the stroke and after.

The day she came over, we chatted and laughed as if no time had passed—part and parcel of a true friendship. While Ashley and I caught up, Paul went down to the basement for Dominic's physical therapy session. I could hear laughter and clapping every once in a while, and it felt weird for me to be upstairs while they were doing therapy downstairs. It was the first session of physio I hadn't participated in.

Afterward, they came upstairs and Paul said Dominic had done something for the first time.

"What did I miss?" I asked.

The PT looked at Paul with a smile. Then Paul looked at me and said, "Let's see if he'll do it again." I tried not to get too excited. There were many things he was currently working on, such as standing up from sitting on his own, pulling himself to stand, standing independently for longer than twenty seconds, and cruising along furniture. The PT set Dominic up and supported him, and he tried to take steps on his own. He took one independently then went to take the second one and started to fall to the side. I thought that even one step independently was a great success.

But Paul stopped me from cheering too much. "No, wait, let's try it again."

"JUST TELL ME!" I pleaded, after a few more tries.

Paul smiled and finally said, "He walked on his own." He'd taken four solid steps before falling to the side, and he'd done this three times during the session. I was so elated I forgot that I'd missed seeing it myself! Paul seemed slightly deflated that Dominic wouldn't "perform" on command, but I said that it was fine, he'd end up showing me at some point.

Christmas Eve was an emotional night. We were at Paul's parents' house for our traditional dinner when Paul told his family about Dominic's walking breakthrough. He apologized for not telling them right away, saying he hoped they'd get to see it for themselves. That day, Dominic cruised along the couches and coffee table and walked well with someone holding his hands but didn't walk or stand without support. Lorren beamed with pride as she explained that she was helping to teach him to do these things—always the doting, maternal big sister. The entire family was supportive and cheered them on.

During dinner, Paul's niece and nephew suggested we go around the table and share our goals for 2019. When it was my turn, I said I was hopeful that Dominic would continue to make gains in his recovery, including walking, and that I had plans to grow my private practice, which I'd be starting in the new year. Paul also had goals around Dominic's recovery and was writing the exam to become a licensed electrician. When it was Lorren's turn, she said, "I hope Dominic will be my best friend, and that he won't need to go into the basement for therapy anymore."

I immediately broke down into tears, as did Paul. I looked toward the corner of the room to hide my face, as I didn't want Lorren to think I was upset about her answer. It wasn't just the beauty in what she'd said that made me cry, but the heartbreak. It was glaringly obvious in that moment that Lorren had been as impacted by what had happened as we'd been. She was standing in the shadow of her brother—and doing so in the most empathetic and mature way. She wasn't upset, she didn't seem jealous, but she knew how important we all thought Dominic's recovery was and shared our sentiment. She'd just shown, yet again, that she was the sweetest big sister. It was the kindest thing I'd ever heard come out of a three-year-old's mouth.

I felt like the worst mother. How could I have neglected her so much? I hadn't even included her in my goals for 2019. Later, Paul and I acknowledged the sick feelings in our stomachs. We were so in awe of our daughter and wanted to make a better effort to show it. We decided to spend Boxing Day celebrating how amazing she was—just Paul, me, and her. One day wouldn't make up for the months apart or the number of hours in a day spent on Dominic, but it was a start. When we told Lorren about Adventure Day, she was more excited about it than any Christmas present she opened.

We spent Christmas Day at my parents' house with some cousins and my brother. It was a fun day, but the kids were exhausted from being up so late on Christmas Eve. After a good nap (for Paul, Lorren, and

Dominic) everyone was in better spirits. We played Christmas Piction-ary—Lorren played for the first time too—and the day felt joyous and hopeful. It provided me with a renewed sense of strength.

The next day, Adventure Day, started with taking Lorren on her first train ride into the city. My mom had arrived at our place early that morning to babysit Dominic. When we got to the station, we found a parking spot and then quickly bought a ticket while running to the plat-form just in time to get on the train. Lorren loved the hustle and bustle. She smiled and ran as fast as her little legs could go. On the train, she picked a seat near a window. It was a great day to commute downtown with a toddler for the first time—it was the day after Christmas and the train was nearly empty.

She stared out the window for most of the twenty-five-minute trip, asking us questions about where we were and what we were passing. When we traveled past my brother's condominium and our first house, Lorren waved and tried to say hello to passersby. She laughed several times, and it was like listening to pure, innocent excitement. Paul and I realized we hadn't heard this from her in a long time. She was elated.

In the city, we walked through Union Station showing Lorren different landmarks and explaining how many people walked through these halls every day. Next, we went to Ripley's Aquarium, located next to the CN Tower, which Lorren was fascinated by. We let her pick the restaurant for lunch (all-day breakfast because . . . pancakes). It was such a nice day spent together. We didn't talk about her brother, therapy, strokes, or "boo-boos." Lorren got our full attention, and she loved the adventure as much as we did. Right before my eyes, my little girl wasn't so little anymore.

NINE

A New Year

STARTING WITH FORGIVENESS

Normally at this time of year, I looked forward to reflecting on all that had passed and setting goals for the year ahead. But this year I couldn't help but feel confused and a little sad. There was so much to be happy and grateful for. Our family had grown stronger, I had some professional clarity, and my pride in and gratitude for my children and life were at an all-time high. None of this would have happened so quickly if it hadn't been for that horrific experience on January 26 and the path that followed.

And yet, I was reminded that I couldn't set goals for recovery. I couldn't place those kinds of expectations on my child as I would on myself. The idea of living with question marks was still unsettling. I really didn't know what to do with this—how to accept it and continue moving forward. Paul and I would talk about it occasionally and validate each other's insecurities surrounding the future. There was no solution, and the problem-solver in me had a difficult time reconciling this.

On December 30, 2018, two of my best friends—Nikita and Ashley—and I decided to do some serious goal-setting, something I typically loved to do. *Maybe this will help me refocus and cheer me up,* I thought. We'd done this together periodically in university and graduate school. We'd write down a ten-year vision and then work backward, often detailing one-, five- and ten-year goals in different realms of life. The first time I set goals, it was part of my training at an athletic apparel store I worked at through graduate school. In my ten-year vision, I was opening a private practice, working part time, finding balance, raising a couple of kids, living in a three-bedroom house, not living beyond my means, etc. It was a lovely little picture. Realizing that I'd achieved a lot of that vision, I felt proud of myself. I was ready to create a new vision, which was an exciting thought. This year, however, the vision experience would be very different.

The three of us settled at the little café recommended by our friend, got ourselves lattes, and got to work. The goal-setting was structured around a deep reflection on the past year and then an acknowledgment of achievements, challenges, and untouched goals. After that it was time to set goals for the year to come. I was feeling as though I'd started to get ahold of my guilt and shame, thanks to therapy. I talked to my friends about the "mom guilt" I carried with me. I worked through the shame of wanting to breastfeed exclusively and not supplementing with formula sooner. I talked about the rationale I'd come up with to explain how the blood clot had formed in my child's brain, even though it went against every scientific explanation. I unpacked the thoughts around not waking him up quickly enough to get him to the hospital before permanent brain damage was done. I could finally talk about it without crying immediately. I often told myself that I'd forgiven myself, but I still felt the pang of guilt from time to time. It was much better, yes, but I hadn't released it entirely.

That day with my friends, I was asked to think about one thing that had happened that year that I was upset about and holding on to that I needed to release. I had to write it down, and I had to forgive myself. Then I had to say it out loud. In front of my friends. I knew the medical and logistical facts: I didn't cause the stroke to happen, and I couldn't have possibly known Dominic was having a stroke at the time. But that didn't matter—that was logical understanding. It wasn't emotional forgiveness.

When it was my turn to speak, I opened my mouth and immediately broke down. I barely got the words "I have to forgive myself" out before tears streamed down my face. I said it over and over. "I have to forgive myself for thinking I caused the stroke to happen. I have to forgive myself for thinking that I thought something was wrong when I was pregnant. I have to forgive myself for listening to the doctors and nurses who encouraged me to breastfeed exclusively. I have to forgive myself for not waking him sooner that morning. I have to forgive myself to move forward."

Nikita sat there, eyes wide, and when I was done, she said something unexpected. "Jen, I didn't know you felt this responsible for the stroke. I didn't know you believed so strongly that you caused this to happen."

Dumbfounded, I replied, "Are you sure I didn't say this? I feel like I talk about my guilt all the time."

"Not like this. Not to me."

That was an eye-opener. If I hadn't said it to her . . . I hadn't said it to anyone. That moment, that confirmation that I'd just shared my guilt in such a raw way, was a release. I felt a bit of weight lift off my chest. I could take a deep breath. It had been a long time since I'd felt able to.

That day, I realized it wasn't guilt that I'd been holding on to—it was shame. Guilt is related to an action or inaction. Shame embodies who we are. The events of January 26 fed into how I saw myself as a mother, wife, friend, daughter. All this time I'd thought I'd come to terms with it (and in a way I had), but I'd never released it. I'd never talked about forgiving myself for even having those thoughts.

Feeling physically lighter, I was in no way "cured" but had a new sense of liberation. I texted Paul while I was still out with my friends and thanked him for holding down the fort so I could be out for almost five hours to do this. It felt like exactly what the doctor had ordered.

After a quiet New Year's Eve, I started 2019 continuing to attend therapy and exercise regularly because it made me feel good physically and, more importantly, gave me emotional clarity and balance. I made a conscious decision to try to see the positive in things while also acknowledging the difficulties. No more "this" or "that." No more all or nothing. Gratitude would be a daily habit—something that I'd make an overt effort to express not just to those around me but to myself as well. I knew it wouldn't be easy, and that some days it would be a lot harder than others, but I chose to make this effort to better my life and the life of my family.

In the end, hurting like hell gave me a needed view of my inner world. I acknowledge the pain and the fear. I choose to accept it, even though

I don't like it, and move forward. It's a part of my story, but it's not the entire story. I'm strong, I'm brave, I'm enough.

LIVING WITH QUESTION MARKS

Relinquishing control sucks. Acknowledging how little of it I actually have over my life is infuriating and scary. I crave control. Most people who live with anxiety do—control means we can predict fairly accurately what's to come, and therefore we can prepare. No question marks.

But this short period of my life taught me that the rest of it was going to be filled with them.

Trying to control everything was exhausting. It made me bitter, resentful, and angry. I missed out on good times trying to plan for what was coming. As I shared, the moment I reacted to Paul's leaving the light on that night was the moment I realized I didn't want to live this way. I was desperate for control, and I realized it. It was time to practice the action of acceptance.

What helped me was starting small. I wasn't suddenly going to become a laid-back, spontaneous person. I knew this, so I changed my expectations. I reminded myself frequently that I didn't need to have control—my anxiety simply wanted it. And it was more important to remind myself that regardless of what happened, Paul and I would handle it. I didn't need to know what would happen or how we'd make it through. The mantra from all those days ago in the hospital came back:

We are going to be okay, even if this isn't.

Unpacking where my need for control came from was important. I
didn't really want to have control for the sake of power—I wanted to
feel safe. I had to work toward reminding myself that I was safe even
when I didn't know what was coming. The evidence was showing me
that even when things went sideways, I'd find a way to make it work.
I'd find a way to survive and grow and be happy. I needed to trust that
I could continue to do this. That we were all going to be okay. It took a
lot of practice, but eventually I started to believe it.

So much *can* happen. I control none of that. All I control is how I
respond. The only thing in this world I can control is me. I can choose to
accept the shitty things in life, grieve, forgive myself, forgive the Universe/
God, and move forward. Even when shitty things happen, life is still
pretty darn good. The more I focus on this, the less I need to know what's
coming. It has helped me stay present more often and enjoy life more.

I continue to practice self-compassion. I allow myself to "sit with the
shit," to feel the grief and loss. It's important. It allows me to release
some of that negative emotion. I set aside a time to listen to music that's
cathartic, or to journal—and if tears flow, I let them. I trust that I'm safe
to do so and that I'll feel better after that release.

Grieving when someone is still alive is a real thing. Most parents
envision their children walking down a particular path. When trauma
like this happens, it changes that path's trajectory. Paul and I had to
learn to give ourselves permission to grieve what we thought life would
look like for our family. We're so grateful for Dominic's life, that he and
Lorren are happy and healthy overall, and that we're together. And the
happiness this brings me outweighs the grief of preconceived notions

of what could have been. The reality is, "what could have been" was just a thought. It was never a fact.

ONE YEAR

The anniversary of Dominic's stroke was fast approaching, and Paul and I knew this would be a particularly triggering day. I'd been thinking about it since Christmas. Dominic was growing and developing. Lorren was a doting big sister, and she and I were closer than ever. Reminiscing on all we'd been through in the past year, Paul and I decided that it made sense to celebrate the anniversary. We couldn't control the memories and events that had brought us here, but we could choose to make where we were a positive thing. And so we did.

That day, we finished Dominic's physiotherapy session and then went out for brunch to our favorite greasy-spoon diner nearby—pancakes with chocolate chips for breakfast. After that, I took Dominic home for a nap and Paul took Lorren mini-golfing for the first time, which she loved. When Lorren got back and Dominic woke up, we let them watch a full-length movie, and the night ended with a bubble bath. It was a simple day with laughter and fun. We chose to celebrate how far we'd come as a family.

The weeks leading up to the one-year anniversary of Dominic's stroke were particularly emotional for me. I was constantly feeling tired again and starting to have flashbacks of the day of the stroke and the following days in the PICU. I'd sit down and look at my kids playing and then suddenly remember the early days: sitting in the vinyl chair, my hair and clothes unwashed, caressing Dominic's sweet face, looking at all the tubes coming out of his little body, listening to the sounds of the machines monitoring his vitals. I'd remember the sound of the hospital-grade breast pump that I used every three to four hours around the clock. I'd remember the smell in the bathroom. The sanitizer that was right beside the door to the room and how quickly it became second nature to sanitize my hands whenever I entered or exited.

In therapy one day, I talked about the mantra I repeated to both kids every night before bed: "You are strong, you are smart, you are kind, you are brave, you are loved, you are enough." And this time when I said it, I started to cry. "I don't know why I'm crying," I said to my therapist. "I never cry when I say this to them."

Always straightforward, he replied, "Are you afraid that one day they won't believe you?"

Yup. I knew how amazing my children were, and that they were capable of greatness. But the world can be a scary place. As much as I wanted to see the light and in ways be the light for others, I was very aware of the prejudice that can exist for those who are different from the "norm." I know how much the teasing words of a peer can hurt. I was teased when I was young for being overweight. The thought of my children experiencing this kind of pain caused a hurt that pulsed in the very center of my heart.

"It isn't fair that Dominic has to go through this," I said. I was quick to follow up with, "And I know life isn't fair and sometimes things just happen and they don't make sense and all of that, but I'm still angry and sad that my innocent child has to go through this kind of hardship for no reason." I continued, on a roll. "It isn't fair that my daughter had to take a back seat to her brother because of his needs, or that she's had to learn about physiotherapy, strokes, and occupational therapy at the age of three."

"Yeah," he said, looking at me. "It isn't."

That was it. *That was acceptance.* It wasn't fair, and there wasn't a thing I could do to change it. I could wallow in the despair, or I could choose to find joy anyway. I could choose to be happy. I could choose to acknowledge that I was experiencing a wave of emotion and ride it. I could trust that the emotional waters would calm again.

They did.

I don't want to host pity parties, but I also don't want to pretend as though this isn't hard. I don't have it all together one-hundred-percent of the time. I'm human, a mom, trying my hardest to be a good role model for my children, a supportive partner to my husband, and a strong advocate and clinician for my clients. Some days this happens easily, and other days it's the hardest thing I do. Some days I'm on top of all the tasks, and others I forget to call someone back, or book that appointment, or take the opportunity to help Dominic practice bimanual activities. THIS is what strength is. Not keeping it together, but rather, allowing myself to feel all of it, and trusting I can carry on.

FIRST STEPS

On January 28, 2019, Paul called me from work and told me that he was being sent home at lunch so that he could beat some of the bad weather set to start midday. A snowstorm was blowing in.

When Paul got home, we tried to play the Doggie Game, introduced to us by Dominic's OT. We'd introduce a sock as a dog and have Dominic pet it with both hands. Then we'd put the sock on Dominic's dominant (right) hand and have him pet the doggie with "lefty." Sometimes he'd resist and sometimes he'd play for a few minutes. Afterward, we'd put Doggie to bed and then give Dominic some toys to play with—but he had to use his left hand. This was a form of constraint-induced movement therapy (CIMT).

CIMT is based on neuroplasticity concepts. It forces Dominic to use the muscles and increase awareness of his affected side, which creates new neuropathways in the brain. If forced to use the affected hand, he gains more movement and function in it. We're now doing this kind of therapy for hours and days at a time. At this point, we were doing five- to ten-minute spurts, until we noticed any sign of frustration or waning motivation. CIMT allowed Dominic to go from not using his left hand and arm at all to pushing objects, hitting light switches, and raking rice.

On this day, though, for some reason Dominic didn't seem interested in Doggie. Instead, he looked over my shoulder at a digital art easel we'd set up in the living room and pointed to it while babbling. "Do you want to use it?" I asked him. He nodded. "Okay, walk there." I positioned myself behind him, let go of his hand, and Dominic stood on his own.

This time it seemed different. He had a look of determination on his face.

He took the tiniest step forward and stayed upright. Paul and I were in shock, staring. After Dominic took two more tiny, slow, methodical steps, I said, "Get the camera!"

Thankfully, Paul was able to record what came next. Dominic walked all the way to the art easel, with me scooting behind him cheering him on. He babbled, seemingly talking about what he was going to do when he got there, unfazed by the fact that he was really walking independently for the first time in his life. When he arrived at the easel, he started to play with it, oblivious to his incredible accomplishment.

I was a puddle. I kissed him and kept repeating "You did it!" through tears. He didn't care in the slightest. It's as if he'd always known he was going to do this and it was no big deal. He was only nineteen months and he'd taken his first steps! I'd hoped that he would walk by the age of three. We sent the video to our families, who shared in our excitement. My father-in-law responded by saying, "Today is a new anniversary to celebrate." He was right.

I'll never miss those early days. But they were a pivotal point in our family's growth. Our children showed us that we don't need to have a plan figured out. Things change, bad or unexpected things happens, and no matter what, we're going to be okay.

I felt we were at the end, or rather the beginning of our journey. The calm after the storm. Sure, it would rain again, but the natural disaster that had wreaked havoc on my family had passed.

Or so I thought.

TEN

2020

The summer of 2019 was awesome. We spent a few weekends up at my in-laws' cottage. Paul and I watched our daughter play soccer. Dominic grew more confident in his walking, his social skills began to develop, and he started speaking a few words and short sentences. Things felt as if they were falling into a sweet groove of mundane. We had found our new normal. I'd begun to feel as calm as I had before the stroke. I was working part time for a school board just outside the Toronto area, and my private practice was growing. I took Dominic to his rehabilitation appointments and follow-ups. He was stable. I was happy.

It was time to revisit the idea of a family trip. Paul and I wanted to finally go to Florida. We wanted to enjoy a vacation, to truly sink into our new version of normalcy. Instead of flying, we drove down to save money, and we took my parents with us for support and companionship. We went over the Christmas break, and it was the first time in our lives that we didn't spend Christmas at home.

The trip was wonderful. The drive there wasn't as treacherous as I'd thought it would be with toddlers. (Shout-out to my parents for being on snack duty much of the time.) The weather was warm and sunny most days. I swam with Lorren in the pool daily, and we spent most of our time at the local beach enjoying snacks and drinks, watching Dominic and Lorren frolic in the sand.

For the first time in a while, I went for runs (since the weather in Florida was nicer than at home in Canada). Then I'd sit on the sand and watch the kids play and start to feel life slow down. I worked diligently at being mindful. I listened to the ocean, the wind, the chatter of other families on the beach. I relished gut-busting bouts of laughter shared with family and the friends who were also there.

I also got to witness my children become best friends. Dominic tried to do all the things Lorren was doing. One afternoon while Lorren was showing off her incredible "downward dog" strength and flexibility, Dominic assumed the four-point crawl position. This was something we'd been working on since leaving SickKids. Both his hands were on the sand, and it looked as though he was even bearing a bit of weight on the left side. Again, he was totally unfazed by his accomplishment. He just smiled at his sister as he attempted to emulate her. He was making developmental leaps.

It was exactly what Paul and I had wanted for our family, and it was healing in a way I couldn't have imagined. And as we prepared to leave, we felt ready to return home to our routines. We were refreshed and excited. I had high hopes that 2020 would be the best year we'd had in a long time.

The night before our departure, my sister-in-law called to tell me my grandmother had fallen down the stairs at home. She'd injured her head and hip and was going to the hospital. Adrenaline started pumping. My parents were distraught, trying to decide if they should fly home immediately or accompany us on the drive back. We ended up driving home as fast as we could.

She underwent surgery, which was successful, and was quickly moved to rehabilitation. Despite the rocky start to the new year, I was determined to stay optimistic. This would be the year of balance. After all, I had a plan and a newfound perspective. I felt more equipped than ever.

And once again, the Universe was about to show me how little I really knew.

COVID-19–AND MORE

On March 12, 2020, I drove home from work listening to the news on the radio. The government was shutting down schools for two weeks after March break due to the novel coronavirus, and the prime minister was asking all travelers to return home or cancel plans to go abroad. It sounded like the country was bracing for a tsunami. *Sounds serious* was the only thing I thought.

At this point, I was working for the school board two and a half days a week. My private practice occupied about one and a half days of my week and the odd evening. I was able to work around Dominic's schedule and Lorren's school drop-off and pickup a few days a week. It was hectic, but I was enjoying being productive and working with clients again.

When the pandemic was declared, I naively thought I'd pivot to online sessions with my clients for a few weeks and then return to the office later in the spring. Ha! Within a week and a half of that announcement, we were on a full lockdown. No more childcare help from my parents or in-laws. No more visits from friends or playdates with the kids. No more school. No more in-person rehab appointments for Dominic.

As essential workers, Paul and I continued working. Paul worked outside the home, and I was expected to work at home—managing my job at the school board and entertaining the children. My private clients started to cancel, saying they were going to "wait it out" until in-person sessions returned. *How long is this going to last?* I asked myself, my frustration growing. *And what does it mean for our family?*

By the end of April, we'd found something of a groove. I'd started to see private clients virtually in the evenings and on weekends, when Paul was home. During the weekdays when I worked for the school board, I'd try to set up the kids as best as I could with snacks and activities on the other side of the table/living room so I could be as productive as possible. It was less than perfect, but we were surviving and making do. "It's temporary," I kept telling myself.

And then one day at lunch, Dominic looked as if he were having a muscle cramp on the left side of his body while sitting at the dining table. It lasted just a few seconds. I asked him if he was okay and he replied "Yeah" after a moment.

I tilted my head to the side and looked at him. *That was weird.* It felt eerily familiar. I got a twinge in my stomach.

I told Paul about it when he got home then sent an email to the nurse practitioner at SickKids. Could it have been a small seizure? He'd been stable for so long. Why now? We hadn't changed the dosage of his anti-epileptic medication for over a year. Perhaps it was just a dosage issue. He'd been seizure free for so long that I'd started to believe he'd be able to get off the medication one day. It was one of the best-case scenarios we'd been told about after his stroke.

The nurse practitioner got back to me and said it could be a seizure but probably wasn't. She asked us (as they always do) to get it on video if it happened again. This seemed like an impossible task, as the episode had lasted only a few seconds, and I had no way of knowing when or if it would happen again.

A week and a half later we met virtually with his neurologist for his annual checkup, and I mentioned it to her. The doctor said that what I was describing didn't sound like a seizure but could be, and told me to continue monitoring him. "If it happens again or becomes more frequent, we can schedule an EEG at the hospital and look at revising his medication regime," she said.

Then she went into great detail about what happens if an "epileptic explosion"—a surge in both clinical and subclinical seizure activity—occurs poststroke. They would trial three or more medications, and if more than two failed, Dominic would be diagnosed with medication-resistant epilepsy. At that point, the only way he'd be able to potentially live seizure free would be to have surgery. And given the extensive damage from his stroke, it would be a large surgical intervention. She explained what the surgery entailed and ended with "That's so far down the road, if ever. I want to be honest with you, but I don't think that's where we're headed with Dominic—he's doing so well."

Within a week of that appointment, he was having the episodes daily. They were seizures. I knew it. I felt it in my core. Every time a seizure would start, my body would tense as if I were preparing for a punch to the gut. I'd drop what I was doing or jump out of my Zoom call and try to catch him as he fell. Or I'd try to catch his head as it went flying toward the table during a meal.

He'd come out of each episode after a few seconds, become upset, and need consoling. Lorren didn't understand what was happening. Neither did I. I did my best to remain calm and keep our routines consistent. I was alone with them, and we were on lockdown. I started to keep a tally, whipping out a journal and noting how many he was having in a day. One a day, then four, then ten.

I kept in close contact with his team at SickKids and was finally able to get two seconds of the end of a seizure on video. They set up an EEG for him within a week. The hospital wasn't seeing kids in person except in urgent circumstances. This was considered urgent.

That forty-minute EEG confirmed my fear. It was seizure activity. The doctor identified step one: increase his current medication and add a second one. They increased his Keppra. They added clobazam. No change. The seizures got longer and more frequent. The falls were harder, the bruises worse, the cries more gut-wrenching.

My productivity at work decreased. My stomach was constantly in knots. If I started a task, I had to be sure I was within arm's length of Dominic. I lived constantly on edge, ready to jump to his aid and try to stop injury from happening. By mid-June I was barely able to work during the day. He was having several seizures an hour, all day long. Sometimes he'd fatigue after a longer seizure or a cluster of seizures and would ask to take a nap. Sleep was his only refuge. It was the only time he didn't noticeably seize.

Whenever I try to remember the details of April to July of that year, I can't. I don't remember what I did for work. I know I did it. I know I saw clients, called parents, wrote reports, but I don't remember doing any of it. I remember only the seizures.

I remember the surge of adrenaline I'd feel every time his eyes widened and he went stiff. I remember my panic. The helpless feeling. My guilt. Dominic began falling off the couch during seizures and often hit the hardwood headfirst. We bought a rug. His balance became less steady. He'd go outside and try to run as he normally did and then fall and injure himself. Going outside became an anxiety-provoking activity. I tried to make him hold my hand, but he protested. Our daughter started wanting to ride in the stroller like her brother, or to be held, because she saw how much more attention and care Dominic was getting. The balance I'd hoped for was quickly forgotten.

A third medication was started and made the seizures much worse. He seized more frequently and his speech was nearly nonexistent. He began stuttering so badly he couldn't get out a sentence. I called the hospital in desperation after a week or two, asking them to take him off this drug. He was losing his ability to communicate—his strongest asset. With every failed medication attempt, we got one step closer to surgical intervention being put on the table.

vEEG

The hospital scheduled a twenty-four-hour vEEG (video-monitored EEG) to find out how many seizures Dominic was having in a day. They also wanted to see if there were any subclinical ones happening. At this point, we had to call in reinforcements. We'd been in isolation for two months, and my parents, Paul, and I agreed to expand our lockdown bubbles. I couldn't leave Lorren for twenty-four hours, and Paul felt he should continue working. Taking time off meant no pay, and it seemed likely that he'd need to be off for an extended period if surgery was coming. I agreed. And so my parents came to stay with Lorren.

Dominic hated being held down while the probes were glued to his head. His screaming was shrill, and after a while it became downright aggressive. He was pissed. I would have been too. I tried to explain to him what was happening and why we were doing this in hopes that he'd understand even just a little bit and calm down. As soon as they were done and the covering had been put on to prevent Dominic from pulling off the probes, he was back to his usual happy self, though exhausted from all the crying. We went to his room, and he walked around with his little backpack (which held the computer monitoring his brain activity). A video camera followed him around the room to capture the physical responses to the brain activity. A doctor would go over this report down to the second and determine when seizures were happening.

We weren't allowed to leave the room during the vEEG, as the camera captured him only inside this room, and the doctor needed twenty-four hours of brain activity to match with a visual of Dominic's body. This would help clarify if seizures were clinical or subclinical. COVID-19 protocols were in place, so any time someone came into the room, I needed to put on a mask and do my best to stay more than six feet away. During this monitoring period, my job was to verbally describe what I was seeing as it was happening. The microphones in the room would pick up my voice. I was told this was important because in some areas of the room, the camera couldn't see the patient and therefore it would be my word or nothing.

The day was simple. I'd packed toys and a tablet to watch TV shows on. We had a little dance party to his favorite songs. Whenever he got bored, I did my best to entertain him with something new. He asked to leave the room to go outside several times. Sadly, we were stuck, but we made it work.

The epileptologist came to see me late that afternoon and told me they had enough to go on already but that they still wanted to assess his sleep. The next day, she returned before our discharge time. She explained that Dominic was having at least twenty seizures a day. None while he was asleep. Twenty. Two months ago, that number had been zero. I'd been missing a good chunk of them. Some of them had happened while he was watching TV—he didn't always have a physical reaction.

Dominic's development had totally stalled. Any and all therapies had stopped since March, due to the pandemic, and the virtual and telephone updates weren't helpful. I heard a lot of "let's put that goal on hold since he's not medically stable right now."

I recalled that first conversation with the doctor about surgery. We were one step closer. Once a child fails to respond to three medicines for epilepsy, the chances of a medication working are nearly nonexistent.

ON THE TABLE

Dominic's doctors had warned us about the type of surgery they'd recommend. Due to the size of Dominic's stroke and the damage to a significant amount of brain tissue on the right side, he'd be looking at a total right functional hemispherectomy. Paul and I already knew what a hemispherectomy was. And the prospect was terrifying.

A year earlier, in that glorious summer of 2019, Paul and I watched a documentary on Netflix called *Diagnosis*.6 In one of the early episodes, a young girl who'd been healthy and happy starts having intense and frequent seizures. Her parents are beside themselves. Puzzled, the doctors recommend a hemispherectomy. They explain that this means detaching one hemisphere of the brain from the other, rendering the detached hemisphere totally useless. It means losing whatever function is housed on the detached side of the brain. It typically means the patient wakes up hemiplegic—unable to walk, sometimes unable to talk, etc. It means grueling rehabilitation in hopes of transferring the function from one side of the brain to the other.

The night we watched that episode, I turned to Paul and said, "I cannot imagine, as a parent, having to make the decision to get rid of half of my child's brain. That's horrifying."

Yeah. It was. And now I was about to experience that decision firsthand.

One summer night while out for our evening walk, Dominic started walking down the driveway. Then he started nearly running. He was getting so fast. Then he froze mid-step (one leg off the ground). His body tensed, and he fell to the ground.

"SHIT!" I yelled, as I grabbed him. He started crying immediately and clung to me with great force. I rushed him back to the house to examine him. He had a scrape under his nose and beside his eye. The swelling had already started to close his eye. I grabbed an ice pack and assumed the usual position on the couch. The saddest part was that this was becoming an almost-daily occurrence. Sometimes he was lucky enough to be on the grass, the carpet, or the couch when it happened. Other times he wasn't so lucky.

My thoughts raced. *What kind of quality of life is this? How can he live like this long term? Are we supposed to stop him from doing anything independently? Am I a bad mom for letting him even go outside? Am I a bad mom for wanting to keep him inside? How am I supposed to do anything else when he requires such intense supervision all the time? What if the falls get worse? What if he's damaging the healthy part of the brain when he falls?* I was scared all the time. This wasn't sustainable for him. It wasn't sustainable for our family. I started to worry more about him being deemed inappropriate for surgery than the surgery itself.

A DIFFERENT KIND OF WAITING

Those weeks between Dominic's vEEG and the team's final assessment regarding whether he was a candidate for surgery were brutal. Part of me wanted to hear that this would just go away on its own, that he could grow out of it. Another part of me knew this was magical thinking. I also thought surgery would be the best way to give Dominic a shot at good quality of life. It also wasn't lost on me that if he needed a hemispherectomy, time was of the essence. The younger a patient is at the time of this surgery, the better their outcomes generally are. The more developing the brain has left to do, the greater the opportunity to acquire lost functions and skills.

I thought about having to go back to the ICU at SickKids, then Bloorview for more rehab. I felt nauseated all the time. Dominic would have to endure the world of hospitalization again. Lorren would have to live without us. Paul would have to divide his time between work, hospital visits, and being home alone with Lorren. I'd have to uproot my life, put work on the back burner, leave my home, daughter, and husband again, and assume the role of case manager, advocate, parent, and therapist full time. But I would do ANYTHING for my children to support their well-being. I was preparing to return and make the best of it.

I was in this dichotomy between two truths. I was willing and able to go back to hospital and rehab life. I saw the purpose and understood the value. I also feared and hated the idea. I didn't want to be in the sterile hospital environment where my child and I would have zero privacy. I didn't want to shower in a shared space as if I were living in a dorm. I didn't want people walking in on us sleeping every hour all night long. The luxury we had this time around, though, was the knowledge of what was happening. Paul and I had the opportunity to think about these things and talk about them. I started practicing a form of intentional acceptance. I accepted that this would happen. I didn't like it, but I understood the reasoning and agreed it was the best course of action. *This is temporary*, I told myself. *The wave of emotion will pass.*

The stroke had been so unexpected and shocking. We'd been thrust from a life of simplicity to the medical world and a life of disability—with NO time to process or prepare. This time we were going in with eyes wide open. I could prepare myself psychologically and physically. This time there would be fewer surprises. I could research the surgical procedure, outcomes, rehabilitation plans, and success rate in advance.

The downside was that this time, I was going in already depleted. I questioned my ability to make it through. I was exhausted. I was scared. Did I have another marathon left in me?

Four and a half months into his epileptic explosion, Dominic was barely talking. He was emotionally volatile. He had black eyes, scrapes, and bruises on his left side from falling mid-seizure. He was less steady on his feet. He was tired a lot. The seizures were now a minute long, and he'd make groaning noises during them, as though he couldn't breathe. A doctor confirmed that the seizures were likely affecting his esophagus. Airflow was becoming constricted. Dominic appeared able to hear us during his seizures. Sometimes it looked as though he was staring off at something else, and other times he'd look right at me, eyes wide, scared, focused on my face. I was completely powerless. I'll never forget how his piercing blue eyes looked at me, begging for help. It was torture for all of us.

I'd drop to the floor, wherever he was. I'd console him, tell him it was a seizure and he'd be okay. We were here with him, and it was going to pass. I would pray for it to stop. I would beg God and the Universe, whoever was listening: *Please don't let this last too long. Don't let this hurt him. Let him get through this without further damage. Please let this be the last one.*

I ran on empty. Every morning I'd check the monitor first thing. If Dominic was awake, I'd watch him and jump from my bed to his room when I saw him starting to have a seizure. Sometimes if Lorren got up before me, she'd go into Dominic's room and play with him. Then I'd hear, "Mommy! Dominic is having a seizure!" and I'd run. My body was in a permanent state of tension, ready to jump when needed.

Around this time, Lorren started to ask those questions we knew were coming: "Why does Dominic have seizures?" "When will I have my stroke?" "When will Dominic use lefty?" "How come Dominic can't do what I can do?"

The doorbell rang one morning while the kids and I were reading and playing with cars on the carpet. When I went to the door, it was open, and Lorren was standing just inside the house. She said, "Hi, I'm a doctor who comes to your house. I'm here to see if anyone has had a stroke and maybe seizures?" It was now a game. I couldn't help but laugh thinking of potential playdates where my daughter would whip out neurological terms for a game of hospital. It was adorable and sad.

One night, Lorren came to me out of nowhere and said, "Don't worry, Mom, Dominic is going to be okay." I hadn't said anything about him—I guess she could feel my worry. I hadn't given this girl enough credit. She was so in tune with emotions and had so much empathy for her age. She taught me to have a positive perspective. She inspired me to get back to focusing on my old mantra—we would be okay, even if this wasn't. She reminded me to focus on the positive and live in the present moment.

I continued to do my best to be age appropriate and honest with her about what was happening and what was likely to come. Paul and I researched helpful children's books. I set her up with therapy for siblings of kids with special needs. I also let her ask questions and answered them as best as I could.

Learning more about this surgery took mental stamina and emotional support. The thought of it was scary. The eight-hour operation would require the doctor to remove part of Dominic's skull and then remove the right temporal lobe (and throw it away) so he could reach the midline of the brain. From there, the surgeon would disconnect every electrical pathway between the right hemisphere and the left. From an electrical perspective, he would completely detach the right half of the brain. This meant that after surgery, the right hemisphere could seize all day long, but the electrical impulses would have nowhere to go and there-fore wouldn't affect Dominic. It also meant he wouldn't have access to any healthy tissue or neurons on this side again. This could change the terrifying trajectory he was on—big time. If he wasn't having constant seizures, he'd be able to focus, rest, learn, regain strength, and get back on a path of growing. It also meant new side effects and more disability.

TESTING, TESTING, AND MORE TESTING

A neuropsychological assessment was attempted at the end of July 2020. These assessments are a standard part of the presurgical write-up, and the results are used to determine if someone is a good candidate for surgery. The team at SickKids wanted to assess where the language center in Dominic's brain was. I learned that for people who are right-handed, the language center is generally in the left hemisphere of the brain. This isn't always the case, however. And since we hadn't had the opportunity to learn which hand was dominant for Dominic because of the stroke (children don't show a preference before twelve months), the team wanted more clarity.

They said that due to his age, it would likely take about three hours. Dominic had a seizure that morning before leaving for the appointment. Not an ideal way to start the day, but it was no surprise to me. By the time we got to the assessment, at 9:00 a.m., he'd had three.

He was able to complete fifteen minutes of the assessment before having a seizure in front of the assessors. After that, his attention went out the window. He complained, tried to get out of the chair and walk around, etc. He had two more seizures, and his distractibility and irritability continued to grow. With each unanswered question I grew more fearful. With each blank stare, complaint, refusal, I became more worried about his cognitive status. I wanted to call it quits by the forty-five-minute mark. At an hour and ten minutes in, the assessors did. They said they had enough information to use.

I realized in that meeting just how delayed Dominic's development was becoming. The assessors gave him age-appropriate, simple tasks, such as, "Show me the dog" (on a sheet with pictures of various items). Sometimes he would and sometimes he wouldn't. His brain was so tired and cluttered with the white noise of constant seizures that he couldn't retain information easily. His word-finding was getting worse instead of better. My hope that the seizures would go away on their own went out the window with his attention span that day.

About a week later, Paul and I were scheduled for a virtual appointment to go over the results. We sat at my work "desk" (a folding table in the basement, thanks to the pandemic) and waited. I could feel myself holding my breath. My chest was tight. What were they going to say about his cognition? Was he on par with his peers? Below average? Much below?

The appointment began with a psychologist telling us how lovely Dominic was to work with and that all areas came in average to low average. I took a deep, releasing breath. One of the psychologists said I looked relieved. My eyes welled and I choked back tears. I was both relieved and saddened. On the one hand, even with all the seizures he was within the average to low-average range. This was good. On the other hand, it was clear that these seizures had a pervasive and negative impact on his learning ability and quality of life.

Then came the news we'd been waiting for. They recommended a total functional hemispherectomy. They believed Dominic's language center was in the left hemisphere, which wouldn't be affected by the surgery. They said that in two weeks, they'd be holding an epilepsy case conference with all the specialties involved to discuss the matter. From that case conference, the decision would be finalized, and then we'd be referred to a surgeon. We'd meet this doctor, talk about the procedure, and book a date. This was happening. I felt relieved, happy, sad, and scared.

The nurse practitioner from the epilepsy surgery team had already informed us (when we first started hearing about surgical options) that Dominic was a great candidate for this kind of surgery. She said that she believed strongly that he'd get unanimous agreement/support from the team. Still, to follow protocol, we had to wait for the case conference.

The conference was for hospital staff only, so Paul and I were told we'd be called following the meeting. It was booked for August 7. We were planning to be at the cottage that week with my in-laws (provided we tested negative for COVID-19) for a family vacation. It would be the first time we'd all been together since the beginning of the pandemic.

I kept my phone glued to me that day, waiting for the call. Around 2:30 p.m., Paul and I went to the grocery store while Dominic napped and Lorren played with her grandparents. My phone rang while I was getting into the car. I took a deep breath.

Here we go.

The nurse practitioner started the conversation with an apology, which scared me. Was he not a candidate after all? But no, she was apologizing because they hadn't gotten to discuss Dominic's case at all—a very complicated case had taken up the entire meeting. She reiterated that Dominic was a good candidate and agreed to make a referral to a surgeon, since it would take a few weeks to get an appointment. She assured me that it would go through, that we just had to wait a little longer. I thanked her for calling and tried not to feel discouraged.

We'd been hoping for some clarity, a step forward, but this wasn't it.

ELEVEN

Preparing

Near the end of August, we received confirmation that there had been unanimous agreement—a functional hemispherectomy was in Dominic's best interest. Everyone on the medical team supported this invasive, scary-as-hell surgery. Paul and I had known this was likely, and hearing the words just highlighted the range of emotions we'd been feeling since the neuropsychological assessment.

I decided to take a leave from work. My family doctor had been encouraging this as well, noting how tired I was and how tense my body had become. I told my boss at the school board and informed all my private clients that I'd need to take a break to support my child. August 31, 2020, was my last day.

Paul and I were scheduled to meet with the surgeon on September

14 for a pre-op appointment. I got a call on the thirteenth saying that it would be a telephone call. This didn't sit well with me, so I requested an in-person meeting. The administrative assistant stated that the doctor was seeing only "urgent" cases in person. I got snappy and asked if we could at least have a virtual appointment.

"This man is going to cut out half of my son's brain—I'd like to see his face before the day he does it."

The assistant quickly backtracked and said that she didn't have any details about the appointments, just names and times. She agreed to follow up with the surgeon and advocate for my request. I understood that it wasn't her fault and felt guilty for being rude. Ten minutes later, I got an email with a link to a telemedicine conference set up for the next day. My bluntness had made the point I'd needed it to make.

We decided that Paul would be on the phone with me while I sat at the computer with the doctor, so that Paul could continue working. He'd need to take time off after the surgery, so he needed to work as much as possible beforehand.

About a week before our consultation with the surgeon, I took Dominic for his three-year-old checkup with his pediatrician, who asked me who'd be performing the surgery.

"Oh, I know him," the doctor said, when I told him. "I went to school with him. He's a renowned surgeon. One of the best pediatric neurosurgeons in the world. He's a great guy. You're in good hands." I felt a sense of comfort that someone was so willing to vouch for this guy before I'd even gotten a chance to meet him.

QUESTIONS UPON QUESTIONS

On September 14, my stomach was a mess. I must have gone to the bathroom a half dozen times that morning. I had a list of questions that Paul and I had compiled during our research phase. I wanted Dr. Truscott to know we were serious about our son's health. That we'd been diligent in our research. And I wanted to find out if I could trust this man with my son's life . . . even though I knew I had no choice. In Canada, it's not customary to get a second opinion, or to pick and choose your physician.

When he joined the call, I immediately noticed his calm, stable energy. He told us he'd done over one hundred hemispherectomies throughout his career, and that he'd explain the operation in as much detail as we wanted (which was *a lot*). He said that he'd make an incision on the right side of Dominic's head in a round shape. He'd remove the cranium in this area and proceed to remove the right temporal lobe. After that, he'd access the deep center of the brain, where all the electrical connections between the right hemisphere and the left are located. Very carefully he would, one by one, disconnect all the electrical "wires" between the hemispheres. Afterward, Dominic's right hemisphere would no longer be able to communicate with his left hemisphere—or with anything for that matter.

He explained that in a functional hemispherectomy, the two masses would still be connected by veins, which carry blood through the brain and body. This would minimize possible damage to the good hemisphere in the future. It would also reduce the likelihood of the unusable part of the brain shrinking or becoming one giant scar. This part of the procedure was newer. Historically, hemispherectomies were anatomical. One hemisphere was physically removed from the brain. "It's still done in some cases," he explained, "but less frequently." The whole thing sounded surreal.

Dr. Truscott informed us that Dominic had an advantage in all of this: he was a stroke survivor. His stroke had been severe and therefore, the tissue being removed was so damaged that it might be a bit easier to remove and could speed the surgery up. He said he suspected that Dominic would be out of surgery in about six or seven hours instead of eight.

This uncommon procedure was done about once every four to six weeks at SickKids. More hemispherectomies were performed at this hospital and Montreal Children's Hospital than anywhere else in Canada.

Paul and I had questions about the lasting effects. The doctor was patient and kind as he replied. He told us that one profound difference after surgery would be Dominic's vision—he'd lose 50 percent of it. Everything to the left of his midline (to the left of his nose) would be lost. The occipital lobe housed a lot of his seizures, so the right side would be disconnected. The loss would be permanent.

This meant Dominic would never be allowed to operate a vehicle with current laws in place. He'd never get a driver's license. It meant he'd learn to navigate the world with a much smaller window of vision. Navigation would require more planning and training. Learning to read would look different. It meant another layer of disability. This was hard to hear, especially for Paul, a car guy who loves driving. He'd talked about working on project cars with Dominic in the future and cruising along beloved routes. These dreams were lost in that conversation. I was hurting too but told myself that if we didn't do this surgery and he continued to have regular seizures, he wouldn't be able to drive anyway. To me, driving was off the table either way. I didn't have the same attachment to the idea as Paul.

We were told to expect exacerbated weakness on his left side and a need for rehabilitation after the surgery. Again, Dominic was in the "lucky" category here. His stroke had been so huge that the right hemisphere was damaged and didn't function in the same way as a neurotypical child's. Dr. Truscott said that he wouldn't be surprised if Dominic could move his left side in some capacity right after the surgery, explaining that Dominic's healthy hemisphere had likely already begun taking on some of the right hemisphere's duties. He probably wouldn't be starting from scratch.

"Children who have a history of stroke with secondary epilepsy, like Dominic, are the most likely to reach total seizure freedom from this surgery," Dr. Truscott explained. He guessed that there was an 80 to 90 percent likelihood of total seizure freedom, and that Dominic would likely be able to get off his medications entirely within a few years of the surgery. This idea alone sounded like a dream. NO seizures? Not one? No meds? I felt myself get hopeful for the first time in a long time. Those were good odds. Really good odds.

I had questions around education and employability. My big-picture thinking was shining through. Dr. Truscott told us he'd performed a hemispherectomy on a patient Dominic's age years ago, and that he'd just received word that the youth had graduated from university. "It's really up to Dominic what he can achieve."

I felt optimistic. We could all work hard. We could all overcome challenges. Dominic had a chance at a beautiful, albeit different, life.

Paul and I thanked the doctor for taking the time to speak to us and for agreeing to a video chat. Before leaving the call, he said he expected the surgery to happen within the next three weeks, near the beginning of October. That was soon. Things were getting REAL. But I wanted to get through this part of the journey as quickly as possible, kind of like ripping off a Band-Aid. Dr. Truscott said we might have a date by the end of the day or the following day.

When I hadn't heard anything by the next day, I, of course, called the office to follow up. I'd realized quickly when we started engaging with medical personnel that callbacks are required. Our kids are everything in our own lives, but they're just one of many in the medical field. Initiation of communication typically falls on the parent or caregiver.

We didn't get a date for another week. I'd emailed the nurse practitioner in a panic one night, fearing that if Dominic didn't get the surgery ASAP, the seizures would spread from the right hemisphere to the left. If that happened, the surgery would be less likely to be successful and damage would be done to the half not impacted by the stroke. Sensing my tension, she ended up calling Paul back before connecting with me. She told Paul she knew I was stressed out and felt that I was panicking. She then called me and said the same thing. She validated my feelings about how hard this time was and assured me it would get easier. She said for seizure activity to become pervasive and move from a localized location to the entire brain takes years. One month of waiting wouldn't likely make a difference for Dominic.

We finally got the call on September 24. Surgery had been set for Monday, October 4, at 8:00 a.m. We would have to get Dominic swabbed for COVID-19 on the Friday morning and would be required to self-isolate after the swab to make sure we didn't expose him to any viruses, especially COVID-19. A second wave was starting in Ontario, and we knew that the sooner he got this surgery done, the better. There were rumblings around the province about preplanned surgeries being canceled unless deemed critical or urgent. I followed up with the nurse practitioner to find out if Dominic's case fell within the urgent category, and she said it did. Unless ICUs were full, Dominic's surgery would go ahead.

In preparation, we started reading books to our children about characters who go to the hospital for a medical procedure. We told both our kids that Dominic was going to have an operation that would help him to not have seizures anymore. We weren't sure how much they understood but felt it was important to give them age-appropriate, honest information. In my work, I'd seen that when children and youth aren't given information about something, they often come up with details on their own. This leaves room for fear and anxiety to fill out the stories in their minds. We didn't want that for our kids. We could handle the conversations about big emotions, and I felt this was a great opportunity to practice articulating how we were all feeling.

HAVING IT ALL

Growing up, I was taught that women could "have it all": a career, a family, and a social life. This was drilled into my head. I was also told that I had to work harder than my male counterparts to get the same jobs or make the same money. No sweat, right? (Ha.) Being faced with the realities of being the primary caregiver for a child with special needs made these expectations heavier. SO heavy that I had to put down certain things. I had to let things go. It was hard. It was deflating. And it was disappointing.

I learned that it isn't about "having it all." It's about being content with what I have. Certain seasons of life simply call for a different focus. We cannot give one-hundred-percent effort to multiple areas at the same time. We must focus our attention on what really matters in each moment.

Everyone was supportive and understanding of my need to take time away from work during this season, so to speak. I, on the other hand, felt as if I'd lost a major part of myself. I'd built that private practice over two years. I'd FINALLY gotten to my goal number of clients in a month. I'd pivoted from in-person to online/telephonic counseling. I'd been taking great pride in helping others through their challenges and struggles. It was also the only break I had from my parent role. The only time that I didn't have to think about syringes and pills. That I didn't need to jump to grab a falling toddler. That I didn't have to worry. The grief was intense. I'd lost a part of my life that had given me a sense of autonomy, purpose, productivity, accomplishment, and more. I was no longer supporting my family financially. The goals my husband and I had wanted to achieve were being forgotten about.

Historically, I would have told myself to suck it up and focus on the kids. Focus on the task at hand. This time, I held some space for myself to grieve and feel. Logically, I knew I was making the right decision for my family and for me. I balanced the feelings of failure around not being able to "hang in there" at work until his surgery date with acknowledging my need for a break. Honoring that need. Knowing that if I were speaking to a client in this situation, I'd be recommending the same thing. I chose to live authentically and practice what I'd been preaching. There was a lot on my plate (and in my head) this season. I had very little control over any of it. The one thing I could remove from the load was work, so that's what I did. I couldn't think of putting the responsibility of caring for Dominic on anyone else.

Still, I felt guilt and shame. *If I step away from my career, I won't be offering financial support to the family. I won't be living up to my expectations—I won't be embodying an independent, self-sufficient, and accomplished career woman, and I won't be setting an example of that for my kids, which I want to do. If I go back to work, I'll miss out on being there with them, on providing therapeutic support and caregiving. I'll feel guilty for asking someone else to care for them. They're my own.* It was a never-ending cycle. No matter which route I'd taken, I would have ended up holding guilt and shame around it.

What was different this time compared to when Dominic had his stroke was that I gave myself permission to slow down instead of trying to power through until a breaking point.

Throughout the journey, I realized that all we can do is accept each day as it comes. I could acknowledge that I was doing the best I could.

Sure, some days 100 percent looks impressive: I get everything on my to-do list done, I work, I engage with my children in a meaningful way, I incorporate strong therapeutic activities that help Dominic in his recovery, and I get some time with my husband and myself. Other days, 100 percent effort is needed just to get to bedtime. The TV is on for hours. Mac and cheese is served for dinner. No one gets bathed. These types of days used to feed my negative thoughts about being "less than." I'd think I hadn't done enough. Then I realized that my effort had been the same all along. It was my effort that mattered, not just the output. Those days happen, and it's okay.

SEPTEMBER 30

One day the week before Dominic's surgery, I woke up at 6:15 a.m. Paul was already at work. I looked at my phone (bad habit) and saw that Paul had sent me a text asking me to call him—there'd been a COVID-19 outbreak at his workplace. A guy on his team (who ate lunch in the same room as Paul) had tested positive, and his site had been shut down. Paul was in line waiting to get tested when I spoke to him. He'd have to self-isolate for two weeks or until he received a negative result.

Shit. Fuck. Seriously? We decided it would be best for Paul to isolate in the basement. We couldn't risk anyone getting sick. He came home after his test and went straight into the basement. I'd drop off food and beverages at the bottom of the stairs and he'd open the door and grab it after I was back upstairs. I disinfected the banister, doorknobs, stairwell, etc. I cleaned anything he'd touched before going to work that morning. I was already stressed out waiting for the surgery, and now I had the added fear of a COVID-19 exposure jeopardizing it. Not to mention I was now flying solo with the kids. It took all of half a day for resentment to show up. Paul had been exposed, and his "consequence" was being locked in the basement to watch TV and play videogames for however long it took to get his result. All while I brought him food and drink. Seemed like a vacation to me!

I had to remind myself (multiple times) that he hadn't chosen to be down there. He hadn't wanted this to happen. It was terrible timing. By Wednesday night, though, I was spent. He wasn't symptomatic, so I asked him to come up for an hour, masked and keeping a distance, to help with some housework. He agreed.

And then came Thursday, September 30. Everything was fine that morning. We went for a walk with the stroller—Dominic donned a child's rugby helmet whenever we went outside, in case he fell. But that afternoon, when Dominic woke up from his nap, he felt warm to the touch. I took his temperature immediately. It was 39 degrees Celsius. My heart rate and blood pressure immediately rose. My back started to seize. *How is he sick?* Maybe he was just hot from being under his blanket during his nap? I took off his shorts and let him hang out in a diaper and a T-shirt, but he seemed a bit more lethargic than usual.

His surgery was in jeopardy. The pre-op package we'd received in the mail stated that we were to contact the office if our child developed a fever within two weeks of the surgery. Over the next few hours, the fever didn't break, even with Tylenol. It went down to about 38 then shot up to 40. I asked Paul to come upstairs because I was worried. Fevers make children more susceptible to seizures, and his threshold was already so low. I needed help. And if Dominic was already sick, it no longer made sense for Paul to isolate.

After dinner, Dominic was sitting on the couch watching a show when he started to seize. This was a seizure unlike any he'd had before. His body shook uncontrollably. His arms flailed. His eyes rolled to the back of his head. He drooled and wheezed. His face turned reddish purple, as if he couldn't breathe. Lorren, not realizing what was going on, said he looked funny and chuckled.

"THIS IS NOT FUNNY!" I yelled. "HE'S HAVING A TERRIBLE SEIZURE!"

She immediately stopped speaking. I called out for Paul to get the Ativan, Dominic's rescue med. This seizure wasn't stopping fast enough. Paul and I were both shaking. He grabbed the Ativan while I dialed 911 with one hand on Dominic. I placed the med on my finger and was about to put it in his mouth when he started to calm. About a minute had passed. I could feel my pulse beating in my neck. I could feel adrenaline moving from my head to my fingertips. My legs felt wobbly, and I was nauseous.

I canceled the ambulance and called the neurologist on call at Sick-Kids instead, who agreed I should bring Dominic in for observation to see if they could find out what was causing the fever in the first place. I figured that at this point, surgery wasn't happening.

In the car, Dominic was dazed but awake, having not fully recovered from the seizure. He was immediately tested for a urine infection, and his lungs were checked. They were clear. I explained that he was due for a COVID-19 test the next morning at 8:00 a.m., so the doctor in the emergency room decided not to swab him, since it would expire before his surgery. I asked the doctor if he would still be able to have the surgery on Monday.

"I'm not able to make that call," she said. "The surgeon will have to decide."

The next morning, Dominic still had a low-grade fever and Paul received his result—negative. That was a relief. If Paul was negative, Dominic didn't have COVID-19, since he hadn't been exposed to anyone else. We stayed on top of the Tylenol and ensured he wasn't overly dressed.

Around 1:00 p.m., I got a call from Dr. Truscott. He apologized and told me that they couldn't proceed with the surgery as planned, explaining that it wasn't wise to operate on someone who was unwell. It could negatively impact Dominic's recovery.

I got it. It made sense. And I hated it.

All the lead-up. All the mental prep. For nothing. I asked if he knew when a new date would be provided, and he said we'd hear back the following week. Paul was visibly pissed off. I tried to rationalize with him. It sucked. There was no denying that. He was right to feel discouraged and upset. I did too. And I acknowledged that this was the right decision. Sometimes the right decision feels like the worst one. He agreed logically, but the emotional piece wasn't quite there yet.

The following day, Dominic no longer had a fever and was smiling and laughing again, but he'd developed a rash—tiny bumps on his chest and back. I looked it up and learned that a viral infection called roseola commonly occurs in toddlers. I tried to determine the cause, confused about how he could have gotten it. Then I read that stress can cause it. We had him checked out by his pediatrician, who agreed it was roseola and that it was quite benign. He said it would heal on its own. Within a few days Dominic, was back to his old self. Now we just had to wait for a new surgery date.

THE NEW DATE

We got a call Tuesday, October 5, and were informed that the surgery had been set for Friday, November 6. A month away. It felt like a year. I asked if there was any way to get an earlier date, but the woman on the other end of the line said that the hospital was trying to catch up on many postponed surgeries from the COVID-19 shutdown in the spring. I said I understood. And again, logically I did, but I was frustrated. Another adjustment. More bated breath. More waiting.

Paul and I decided that he should return to work, and that we'd quarantine a week before surgery. Lorren went back to school for a couple of weeks. We spent Thanksgiving at Paul's parents' cottage just the four of us. We needed space. We needed a change of scenery. It was a wonderful weekend. Dominic had only one seizure the whole time. We went on walks, played in the leaves, watched movies. Sat around. It was good for our souls.

I'd noticed that since Dominic's tonic-clonic seizure, his seizures had calmed significantly. He was barely having any compared to the week before. Could this be a sign? Was he growing out of the seizures? Was he not supposed to get the surgery? All the questions started flowing. The confidence I'd felt in our decision to move forward with surgery crumbled. I knew his medical team had unanimously recommended it. I also knew that epilepsy is so unpredictable and can go dormant for days, weeks, months, even years and then rear its ugly head again, worse than before.

I reached out to the online community of parents of pediatric epilepsy surgery patients asking if something like this had happened to others. Pretty quickly I learned that it was quite common for kids to go through a "remission" period after being ill. It's as if the brain calms itself to focus on healing and therefore seizures become minimal. So many parents acknowledged that they, too, had questioned surgery during these periods of stability. Not one parent regretted pursuing surgery. Not one had canceled theirs.

I also consulted with the nurse practitioner working with us, and she confirmed that a silent period was common. "It doesn't mean he's outgrown the seizures, and it doesn't mean another epileptic explosion is off the table," she said. "In fact, once one explosion occurs and is untreated by meds, it's likely to happen again, timing unknown."

That wasn't a risk we were willing to take. Knowing the detrimental impact these seizures had on Dominic's development and emotional stability, and on our lives, we weren't willing to wait around and see what would happen. The surgery was time sensitive. We moved onward.

At the end of October, I once again got a call from the surgeon's office. The date had been changed again. I immediately tensed. "What?

When is it?"

"Not a big change, just two days earlier."

Finally, some good news. It would be on Wednesday, November 4, at 8:00 a.m. Now we were only ten days away. The countdown was on.

That Halloween was abnormal, since we were in the second wave of the pandemic. Trick-or-treating wasn't happening, and I was grateful, given that we were in isolation. The kids dressed up in their costumes and knocked on the bedroom doors. Paul and I hid behind them and pretended to be different people with every knock. It might not have been the most creative Halloween, but the kids liked it and the candy was enjoyed by all.

We spent those few weeks leading up to surgery as a family. We went apple-picking on a farm, spent time at the cottage, watched movies, and just enjoyed each other's company. I soaked up our time as a foursome knowing that we'd soon be apart for an unknown period of time.

The night before the surgery, Lorren said goodnight to Dominic and wished him good luck. We assumed she'd be asleep when we left the next morning, as we had to be on the road by 5:15 a.m. Lorren hugged her brother tightly and told him she loved him. "I hope you'll be home soon," she said.

So did I.

TWELVE

Hemi Day

I was steady and calm when I woke up the morning of the surgery. Paul and I got up at 4:30 a.m. to give Dominic his morning meds, as directed by the hospital. Only clear fluids had been allowed since midnight, and he wasn't allowed to have anything to drink for three hours before surgery. Lorren heard us getting ready and woke up to give Dominic several more kisses and hugs.

My parents, who'd slept over the night before so they could look after Lorren, also hugged Dominic. "Everything is going to be okay," they said, crying. I stayed stoic, but at this point my stomach was in knots. I wanted to throw up. I could feel the pulse in my veins from my chest to my fingertips. This was it. It was happening.

We got in the car and headed downtown. The plan was for Paul to drop us off. Due to COVID-19 protocols, only one parent was allowed to be inside the hospital until the child was in a room. We decided I'd go in for the pre-op. Paul downloaded a movie to watch while he waited the two hours before Dominic went into surgery. He said he was fine with the decision for me to go into the hospital, but I knew that it would be hard, sitting in a parking garage waiting for me, not getting to be with his little boy. I thought it would feel like the longest few hours of his life. He confirmed this later that day.

In pre-op, Dominic and I played games and had tickle fights, and I consoled him when he became agitated or had a small seizure. I let him watch *Tayo the Little Bus* on my phone. By 8:00 a.m., we'd gone through the entire spectrum of emotions.

Around 7:30 a.m., the anesthesiologist introduced himself and asked me a few questions about Dominic and his history with anesthesia. He also asked if I wanted to walk Dominic into the operating room. "Absolutely," I said. I didn't want to let Dominic go into that room alone. I knew that he didn't totally understand what was happening that day, but he knew something was up. The doctor explained that throughout the pandemic, they'd been trying to limit the number of people in the operating suite but that he'd ask for an exception to be made given Dominic's age and the significance of the surgery.

Thankfully, I got the all clear to carry him to the operating room. I gowned up, put on gloves (I already had a mask on), and carried him down a hall with windows on one side and doors on the other, following a nurse. It felt as if I were moving in slow motion. I looked around, trying to take in the sterile sights. The bright morning light, the whiteness of the walls, the doors opening and closing. Without thinking, I held Dominic a little closer and whispered into his ear, "Repeat after me: 'I am strong, I am brave, I can do anything.'" And he did.

The nurse opened the door to the operating room. It was stark, and brighter than I'd imagined. It was also smaller than I'd envisioned. There were several people in there, but I was focused on the bed and my boy. They asked me to place him onto the bed. I kissed Dominic and told him I'd see him when he woke up. I told him I'd be with him always.

"I want to go," Dominic said. I could see he was getting scared. I was scared too.

The anesthesiologist said hello to Dominic and also asked me to put him on the hospital bed. Finally, I did. I hugged Dominic while the anesthesiologist put the gas mask on him, and I told him how much I loved him, how brave and strong he was. Dominic was half crying.

The doctor quickly asked me to move my head, saying I'd end up inhaling the gas myself and pass out. I lifted my head up and to the side but continued talking to Dominic and stroking his arm and head. I told him I loved him, that he was safe, and that he would go to sleep and I'd see him when he woke up. Within seconds, Dominic was fast asleep.

A nurse came up to my side and said into my ear, "I'm here to make sure Dominic is comfortable—that's my only job during surgery. He's not going to remember any of this. He's asleep now. We are going to take good care of him, I promise."

Instant tears. It was happening. There was no more waiting, no more denying what was going on. It was time for me to walk away from my baby, who was lying on an operating table, and hope that the team around him would keep him alive.

Several doctors and nurses asked if I was okay, as they could only see the redness in my eyes and the tears rolling down behind my mask. "I'm just nervous," I said, trying to sound brave. "I've never left him like this before."

The nurse passed me to another staff member, who walked me back to the pre-op area so I could take off the gown and gather my stuff. The tears flowed for a few more minutes. Staff who passed continued to ask if I was okay. I always said I was. And I meant it. I felt weak and sick and terrified, yet strong and calm.

Because the surgery was lengthy, I was encouraged to leave the hospital and walk around. Paul and I had booked a hotel room because parents couldn't stay bedside in the ICU and the Ronald McDonald Room was closed due to the pandemic. I called Paul, and we met at the hospital's entrance. Then we walked around the building over and over. I was quiet; so was he. After about an hour, we decided to try to settle in at the hotel.

To say this was hard seems like a bit of a joke. That day, we said goodbye to whatever was left of half of Dominic's brain. It felt cruel. Still, we knew this was what our son needed. We knew his medical team was among the best in the world. We were confident and trusted that they had his best interests at heart. He was in capable hands. In that, I felt confident and calm, even though I was fearful. I knew we could do this.

The journey leading up to the surgery had been so heavy. So difficult. I also knew how strong we were. Strong as a family and individually. *We will get through it*, I thought. I knew we would. I chose to believe that. I had asked our family and friends for support, well wishes, positive vibes, and prayers going into surgery, and I believe my ability to focus on this positivity with laser sharpness was in part thanks to them.

Paul and I got to our room and set down our bags. The hotel was quiet due to the pandemic. I told Paul I wanted to do some meditating to calm my nerves. He nodded and sat quietly on the bed. I sat down on the desk chair and put on my headphones. I slowed my breathing. I envisioned my child on that table. Then I envisioned a warm, white, golden light. The more I focused, the brighter the light got. I then visualized this healing light wrapping around not just Dominic and the surgeon, but also Paul, Lorren, the nurses, the aides—everyone. I pictured the surgery being super successful. I sat with that image for about five minutes. Thoughts of catastrophe passed by for a few seconds, but I was determined to stay focused. I'd been practicing meditation for a while and felt that doing so had set me up for success on this day.

After I finished, I read through the numerous comments from family and friends on Instagram. So many of them, our nearest and dearest as well as people we didn't see often or talk to much, commented that they were praying—not just for Dominic but also for the hands that were healing him. Dozens of people were sending strength, love, peace, and healing. In a time when I felt exhausted, depleted, and scared, the positivity, strength, and love from others carried me through. I physically felt it. I knew this would be a long day, and there was a long journey ahead, but for the first time in a long time, I felt as if I had the energy to continue. I cried many gratitude-filled tears that day.

About two hours before the expected completion time, I told Paul I'd go back into the hospital and wait. Paul agreed to wait at the hotel. We'd both be allowed in once Dominic was in a room in the ICU. I sat in a waiting room filled with parents, all of us at least six feet apart from each other. All waiting for our child's doctor to walk through that door and say what we desperately wanted to hear: "It went well."

I looked around. Every parent was doing their best to stay occupied. The room was eerily quiet. Every once in a while, a doctor would come into the room and ask to speak to someone. A parent would get up, looking tense. Then came a wave of relief when the doctor would say, "All good, let's talk." The doctor would usher them into a small room to speak about specifics in private.

Around 2:30 p.m., Dr. Truscott came into the room. With his gown and mask, I barely recognized him. He looked at me and hesitated. Turns out that with both of us wearing masks and having never actually met in person, he had difficulty recognizing me as well. I got up and walked over to him, and he said the words I was desperate to hear: "The surgery went well. We're just finishing up now." Joy and relief flooded me as I took a deep breath and followed him into that little room. I asked if I could call Paul, so he could be part of the conversation, and Dr. Truscott said yes. I put Paul on speakerphone so he could ask questions if he had any.

"I was able to make all the disconnections," Dr. Truscott said. While opening the cranium, he'd found the temporal lobe, which was essentially "goop" being held together by scar tissue. "No amount of medication was ever going to stop those seizures. The brain was just too damaged by the stroke." Simple, matter-of-fact information that I will never, ever forget. At that second, any remaining self-doubt dissipated. We'd made the right choice. We'd made the only choice that would give our son a chance at seizure freedom.

Once Dominic had been settled in recovery, I was called in. He was in and out of sleep, his head wrapped. A tube in his skull was filling up a bag with drainage. I was told this extraventrical drain (EVD) would be in there for a few days, removing any excess cerebrospinal fluid to help reduce pressure buildup—the brain was expected to swell as it healed after such an assault. Then they'd remove it and see how the brain adjusted. We'd have to wait and see.

Dominic was out of it the rest of the day, awake for just a few short minutes, nauseous and vomiting. They moved him to the ICU about an hour after I joined him in recovery, and Paul was able to meet us there. We sat, half hanging over the hospital bed, stroking Dominic's hand and telling him how proud we were. The first and biggest hurdle was over. Now he could rest and heal.

Paul and I went to sleep around 9:30 p.m. that night. The plan was to get up around 5:30 a.m., shower, and head to the hospital so that we'd be there before rounds at 7:00 a.m. But around 1:00 a.m., I woke up and called the unit to check on him. I didn't have the luxury of being in the same building as Dominic this time around.

We were at his bedside first thing in the morning and found him sound asleep. The nurse confirmed he hadn't been sick since they gave him the dose of antinausea medication the night before. He started to wake up and was groggy and cranky but alert—a good sign. He moved to the neurology floor later that morning and ended up being across the hall from our original room, where we'd stayed nearly three years earlier. I was reminded of how much had changed since then. I recalled how scared and alone I'd felt. How unprepared and unqualified I'd thought I was to care for my child as I desperately tried to make sense of the future. I never would have imagined we'd be back here for this, and yet I felt stronger and more capable than ever, despite my exhaustion.

POST-OP

The first week was rough. Dominic was sensitive to sound and light, and he spent most of his days asleep. When it was time to eat, he wanted only pancakes and blueberries. When he tried to watch a show, he'd immediately become overstimulated and exhausted, and would often tell us to turn it off. He was demanding, cranky, and short. He wanted us close to him in bed but didn't want us to touch him. Two people in a small hospital bed is a challenge. Two people not touching in one is nearly impossible. I assumed my position every night, cramped up against the bed rail, praying it wouldn't give way, otherwise I'd end up on the hospital floor.

His sensations were in overdrive. His brain had been through a major trauma and was trying to regroup. We encouraged him to sleep. We tried to gently talk to him when he was awake.

A few days post-op, while lying in bed with Paul and eating blueberries, Dominic giggled a little at a joke Paul made. It didn't last long, but I was so happy. He was starting to show glimmers of his personality again, even just for fifteen seconds a day.

One evening a few days after the surgery, I lay in the hospital bed carefully curled close to (but not cuddling) Dominic. He was calm and subdued. All of a sudden, he began to wince and move his arm. I noticed that his fingers looked like sausages. The IV popped. I immediately hit the call bell and requested nursing. As I waited for someone to arrive, I felt useless. His arm continued to swell before my eyes, bigger and bigger. Staff were there within a minute, but by that point, Dominic's arm was three times its normal size. Dominic kept wincing in pain but wasn't full-on crying. It seemed harder for me to hold back tears. The nurses were gentle and kind, and the doctor on call spoke to me afterwards. No one understood what had happened—they'd checked the IV an hour before and it was fine. They removed the IV completely, and we tried to keep his arm elevated so that it could drain. It took about three days for the swelling to go down completely. You'd think I would have been used to hearing that some things happen for no reason, but it still burned to hear it again. The unfairness of it stung.

Despite that event, Dominic continued to make gains each day. The fluid from the tube in his skull seemed to be decreasing in volume and was clearer. About five days post-op, the team tried to clamp the tube to prepare for its removal. Unfortunately, his brain wasn't ready. We saw a regression within hours. He became super irritable, wouldn't stay awake for long, and appeared to be in pain. They reopened the clamp, and more fluid was removed. They said they would keep it open for a few more days but wanted to close it by day seven or eight, as the longer it was open, the more susceptible Dominic was to infection. If his brain couldn't level out the fluid in the brain after this surgery, then Dominic would require a permanent shunt. This would mean another surgery. We were hopeful he wouldn't need it, and thankfully at day eight, the EVD was removed and he seemed to adjust well.

On day ten in hospital, a Saturday, we were told that Dominic would be going to Bloorview on Monday. He was medically stable and ready to start rehab. Paul and I were surprised, and so grateful. This was four days earlier than expected. Dominic had done ten minutes of OT and PT the day before. He'd also grabbed a toy with his right hand and walked (assisted) a few steps from the bed to the door but complained the entire time. It was clear that the week in bed had led to deconditioning.

The on-call physician that weekend told us that we could take him home for the rest of the weekend before heading to rehab. Paul and I thought long and hard about this. The last time we'd been told to take him home, we'd been super anxious and unsure of our ability to care for him. This time felt different. He was older and eating independently, and we had a definitive entrance date. In the end, the opportunity for Dominic and Lorren to be together felt too good to pass up. And so at 4:00 p.m. on Saturday, November 14, 2020, we headed home.

Lorren was elated to see her brother. Dominic would sit up on the couch or play sitting up on the floor for about twenty minutes at a time before needing a solid rest. He napped two or three times per day. We ate a few meals together. We talked to the kids about going to Bloorview again and explained that Dominic and I would be back on weekends, hopefully, if it were allowed (due to the pandemic).

It was a quiet day and a half. And come Monday, we were ready for the next step.

THIRTEEN

Rehab, Covid-19 Edition

We arrived at Bloorview Monday morning at 8:30 a.m. This time I was prepared. I had a foam pad for the hard-as-rock pullout chair, sandals for the shower, toiletries, toys for Dominic, and more. We had a private room (thankfully), and it happened to be next door to the room we'd inhabited during our previous stay.

Location aside, though, things were different this time around. There were no group activities. The pool was closed for most of our time there. The playroom was capped at ten people total, which meant five kids maximum. And our therapy team was made up of entirely different people.

Dominic arrived at Bloorview able to sit up and take a few steps on his own with his ankle foot orthotic before fatiguing. He began doing twenty to thirty minutes per day of targeted therapy, and within three weeks, he was doing nearly two to three hours of therapy a day. His bounce-back was incredible. Dominic continued to shock us. He was showing us that he could get back to his baseline. Maybe he could pass it.

At the intake meeting with the team, at the end of November, Dominic's tentative discharge plan was discussed. The transition coordinator stated that he was scheduled to be discharged on January 11. Both Paul and I wore looks of shock. That was only six weeks away. At this point Dominic had JUST started to engage in therapy fully. He was still regaining energy and a capacity for learning. Right away I expressed my concern. I explained that we'd been at Bloorview for twelve weeks the first time, and that we knew other children who'd had hemispherectomies who'd been at Bloorview for ten to twelve weeks.

"He's young and requires a lot of rest," I said, "which will make the first part of his rehab slower." I continued, saying that given the pandemic, I knew that the moment we got home, rehabilitation sessions would drop from three times a day to two times a week, if we were lucky.

The team listened, and Dominic's therapists came to our room after the meeting to thank me for speaking up. They all supported extending his stay. New policies deemed, as a general guideline, that hemispherectomy patients were to undergo eight weeks of therapy. The date I'd been given was standard and fluid, dependent on how Dominic was doing as an individual. The therapists agreed to advocate on their end as well. After Christmas, we were informed that Dominic had been approved for a four-week extension. This was a small victory for our family.

Dominic's rehabilitation didn't slow down for one minute. Each week he did more than the last. He was growing and becoming more verbal with every interaction. The physiotherapist suggested that we decrease the amount of support his foot brace was offering and allow him to work on building muscles on his left side. She explained that we'd lose a bit of the integrity in his gait form but would increase his muscle mass and balance in the long run. We decided to go for it.

Whenever Dominic was challenged in rehabilitation, he'd protest and shut down, but with repetitive exposure and a lot of different behavior-coaching tactics, Dominic worked toward every single rehabilitation goal the therapists had set for him. He led by example. Therapists loved working with him. Nurses loved coming into our room to see Dominic.

Our son was once again showing us that with focus, determination, a positive attitude, and perseverance, he could—as author Glennon Doyle says—do hard things. We all could.

A HEALING INFECTION

In anticipation of the surgery, I'd looked forward to the time we'd be at Bloorview. I remembered the first time: The gaps in the day when Dominic would nap and I'd binge-watch a TV show quietly in the cot beside his bed. The luxury of not having to cook and clean. The slower pace. The relative quiet—fewer machines making noise, fewer voices on speakers. I'd get an hour break here and there while Dominic was in the playroom. When Dominic napped, I could rest, recharge, take a shower, etc. I had to look after only one child for five days of the week. I exercised. I ate as healthily as possible. And so I'd psyched myself up to use this next block of time at Bloorview to do some healing of my own, alongside Dominic.

But a week and a half into our stay at Bloorview, my own physical pain started. I woke up in the middle of the night with extreme itching in my left ear—the kind of itch that could be scratched until drawing blood. Which I did. Nothing satisfied it. I woke up scratching without realizing I'd been doing it. I thought it was allergies. By the next morning, though, I was in terrible pain. I couldn't hear out of the affected ear at all. It was completely blocked. The pain radiated from my ear up into my skull and down my jaw to the front of my face. I figured it was from the wild amount of scratching in my sleep. Tylenol and Advil didn't touch the pain. It kept getting worse.

Staff would walk in and immediately say that I didn't look like myself. I kept conversations with staff and other families as short as possible. The rest and relaxation I'd planned to give myself during our time at Bloorview quickly became time to store whatever energy I could so that I was able to participate in therapy sessions with Dominic.

Because of the pandemic, local urgent-care centers were closed. I called my family doctor, but they weren't available for several days. Finally, on a Friday night, I ended up in the ER. The doctor who saw me said that there was something in my ear. Gross. He tried to remove it and in doing so, ruptured my eardrum. It sounds worse than it was. The rupture released the pressure and the pain decreased dramatically. I still couldn't hear, but at least the pain was manageable. I returned to Bloorview that Sunday with renewed optimism. Between the antibiotics and the rupture, I was surely healing.

Monday was a solid day. I had a smile on my face (behind my mask) and pep in my step. Dominic was doing amazingly well in therapy, and I joined him in the playroom to show staff how to practice the skills he was learning in therapy. By Wednesday, the pain had returned. And this time it was worse than before. I ended up on another course of antibiotics. I now couldn't hear anything out of my left ear, and my right was muffled at best. I was in pain all day and night. I slept with gloves on to prevent my hands from doing any more damage. I was exhausted all day. I retreated to our room whenever I had a chance and tried to sleep or at least lie down.

This yo-yoing between Bloorview, my family doctor, and the ER continued for six weeks. Finally, on my third visit to the doctor and after my third round of ineffective antibiotics, I was referred to an ENT, who took one look at me and said I had a severe infection. A yeast infection—in my ear. Ew. I'd never had a yeast infection before, and I hadn't known it could show up in other areas of the body. The ENT said it was random, not common, and extremely painful. Once the treatment course changed to address the actual problem, I started to feel better. Back to bubbly rehabilitation-mom life!

A week after that relief, though, the infection returned. My ear was plugged again, and I couldn't hear. I desperately pleaded with the doctor. What was causing this? Was it me? Was I doing this to myself? Could it be my shampoo? Could it be the hospital air? My pillowcase (which I was changing nightly)? I nearly cried as I sat in his office. "You don't understand," I said. "I don't have time to be in this kind of pain. I don't have time to run from city to city between my son's rehabilitation sessions."

"Sometimes these kinds of infections just happen," he replied. "We don't know why."

My "love" for unexplained things is no secret. This rationale infuriated me. I started to reflect on what could have triggered this. I'd had chronic stress for months. I'd listened to countless medical staff offer different recommendations regarding how to treat Dominic. I'd worked hard to give my daughter extra attention in anticipation of my returning to the hospital. I'd listened to clients up until a month and a half before Dominic's surgery. And I'd mentally prepared to take a break and start to heal during Dominic's rehab. My mind had been set on recalibrating in this safe space, away from home and other people. The moment I arrived at Bloorview, my adrenaline levels started to come down, and the stress started to affect my body. It was as if my ears had heard enough and needed a break. Since I wouldn't stop, they made me.

It got to the point where my ears were so plugged that staff had to raise their voices to speak to me. I had to read Dominic's lips on several occasions to make sure I understood what he was saying. Conversation stopped. I no longer had to listen in great depth, as I had for months (actually, years). This was how my body was trying to heal itself—by shutting down what had been most open.

Of course, this is just my interpretation of how things went down, but I strongly believe in the link between mental and physical health. I couldn't heal my heart and mind with my body going at the rate it had been. Only when it shut down and stopped listening to outside noise was I able to start healing in any real way. It was also a wake-up call. Living in a hospital is not a VACATION. Pretending that this was the case was my version of "fake it till you make it." It was certainly a positive change from acute care, but the reality is that living in a hospital wearing a mask most of the day, sleeping on a vinyl board half the size of a twin bed, staying away from all other people, engaging in therapy, showering in a shared space like a student living in residence, seeing and hearing all about different people's experiences with brain injuries, trauma, and crises, and eating whatever scraps my son didn't finish plus a few snacks I packed is NOT a vacation. I hadn't vacated my life. I was back to where a lot of my trauma seeds had been planted.

Once I wrapped my head around that, I started to remove the expectations and plans I had for myself. I stopped putting pressure on myself to be productive during my "breaks." I stopped feeling guilty about not participating in every single therapy session. I started focusing on slowing down. I focused on starting to let go (slightly) and allowing Dominic to work with his therapists more independently. And as a result of this new outlook combined with modern medicine (Thank you, Dr. M.), my infection started to improve.

MIRACLES

That Christmas, Paul had a few days off work. I was still going to doctor's appointments and follow-ups for my ear, so we decided that for the few days he was off, he'd stay at Bloorview with Dominic and I'd stay with Lorren. This is something we never did the first time around. It was a great opportunity to have "girl time." I loved hanging out with my daughter, baking cookies and watching movies.

We all spent Christmas Day with my parents since they were living in our house most of the week (watching Lorren while Paul was at work). It was a much quieter version of our usual Christmases thanks to COVID-19. That morning while I was getting dressed, Dominic and Lorren were having a little photoshoot in front of the Christmas tree when I suddenly heard Paul and Lorren start cheering on Dominic. I walked down the hall and saw that Dominic was holding a Ziploc bag with his left hand and pushing it up against his waist while putting blocks in it with his right hand. A BIMANUAL ACTIVITY! This was the first time since his stroke that he'd engaged in an activity like this. Dominic was so proud of himself, and Paul and I were overjoyed.

That Christmas was one full of hope and optimism. Five weeks post-op, Dominic was showing incredible promise. It felt like a Christmas miracle. Gratitude and positivity washed over me and stayed with me all day, despite the physical pain I was dealing with.

The more I thought about that day and all the other milestones Dominic had accomplished, the more I began to see the real gift I'd been given—the power of perspective. Little things that would have been glossed over, ignored, or, worse yet, missed entirely were now highlighted and celebrated.

Now, whenever Dominic or Lorren reaches a milestone, we celebrate. We have dance parties, we share kisses and hugs. Gone are the days of taking things such as movement, speech, and memory for granted. These are gifts, and we're treating them as such.

That midpandemic Christmas was weird, but also particularly wonderful.

FEELING IT ALL

Toward the last five weeks of Dominic's rehabilitation, I started to physic-ally heal. I went days without excruciating pain in my ear, head, and face. I started to smile under my mask. I took time between therapy sessions to play with Dominic. On sunny days when Dominic was napping, I'd let a nurse know he was sleeping and head out for a walk around the neighborhood for fresh air (because of the pandemic, I wasn't allowed to do this with Dominic). I started listening to music, meditating, and exercising again. I started writing again.

One night while Dominic was in the playroom for an hour before bath and bed, I sat at my computer and listened to music that brought up strong emotions for me. I sat with those emotions with no expectations of processing them or pushing them away. And as I sat with them, I started to see them in a new way. I didn't try to rationalize them away with the "it could be worse" mantra. I just let them be.

I took a slow, deep breath and suddenly, tears were streaming down my face. They were hot, coming fast and furious. Normally I would have worried about families in the adjacent rooms or nursing staff outside hearing me. But on this night, I didn't care. I finally gave myself permis-sion to feel. I must have cried for forty minutes. I cried for my son, who'd been through a hellish ordeal in his short three and a half years of life. I cried for my daughter and how much she'd endured, how much I missed being near her. I cried for Paul, thinking of how hard it must be to be doing this one step removed—going to work and parenting solo with the knowledge that half the family was elsewhere, working on building some semblance of quality of life. I also cried for myself. I finally felt the weight of what I'd been carrying for more than three years.

In those early days, I'd felt that I had no choice but to be positive. I believed I HAD to focus on the bright side and make the best of the situations: *Dominic will recover as best as he can, and that will be the perfect amount. Our family will continue to grow from our experiences.* In this moment, as I sat in my puddle of tears, I realized it had always been a choice. I'd chosen to be positive. I'd chosen to do those meditations and visualizations. I'd chosen to ask questions and learn as much as I could with each additional diagnosis. Now, I finally allowed myself to begin to release all the pent-up grief, sadness, and fatigue that had traveled with me all those years, waiting for their opportunity to be acknowledged.

I thought about the past seven months. The hell that 2020 had brought. The pandemic. The social injustice and systemic racism and inequities. The seizures. The surgery. The fear. The loss of my career. All of it. I didn't understand why the release was happening now, but I wanted to honor whatever I was feeling.

Finally, after forty minutes, I noticed the time on the clock and composed myself to get Dominic ready for bath time. I took a few long, deep breaths. I thanked the sadness. I thanked the grief. I wanted to appreciate the emotions I was feeling. It was in the sadness, grief, and loss that I was able to appreciate the joy, love, and light in my life. I had so much to be grateful for. It was extremely cathartic.

There is something to be learned from intense emotions. So many people still believe that showing sadness or grief is a sign of weakness. They identify these emotions as "negative." That couldn't be further from the truth. Think about how hard it is to admit to yourself and others that you need help. Think about the catharsis of a good cry. It takes strength to allow ourselves to feel the emotions that lie deep within. Once we get honest and acknowledge them, we can validate their importance, process them, and release them. They will still exist, but without that same power and control that they once had.

During the final weeks of Dominic's rehabilitation, I started to connect with other people again. I started talking to other parents. I learned about all the different reasons that had brought us together. I learned that one other child was also there for the second time—a rarity at Bloorview. I started to see my former self in a lot of the mothers I met in that common room.

I still think about these mothers often and send thoughts and prayers of self-compassion and healing to them.

HOMEWARD BOUND

On February 11, Dominic finished his final therapy sessions at Holland Bloorview Kids Rehabilitation Hospital. I'd written thank-you cards for many of the staff who, by now, felt like friends. I wanted to thank people for all their help and support. The village we had around our family was immense, and it wasn't lost on me how fortunate we were to have it.

Dominic didn't seem to care much about our departure. He'd returned to this place unable to walk independently, needing a nap after twenty minutes of therapy, and saying just a few words at a time. He was leaving walking with less support than when he arrived and laughing alongside the therapeutic clowns who sang a song for him and told him how much they would miss him as he walked down the hall toward the elevators.

Paul joined us after work and got us ready to go. He packed up the van while I paused and looked around. I looked out the window from which Dominic would stare at the school buses dropping off and picking up children for the day school located two floors below our room. I looked at the communal shower and bathroom. I looked at the hospital walls, which seemed friendly and comforting. They housed a familiar safe haven. People here understood life with disability. Everything was accessible. I took deep breaths and tried to draw on the strength of this place. I hoped to savor it and take it with me. I knew that the work didn't stop here, that it was beginning. It was time for me to leave the nest and start advocating for my child without the safety net of a multidisciplinary team behind me.

Although I hope to never return to this place, I'll be forever grateful for all it provided my son and family.

FOURTEEN

The Journey toward Healing, Take Two

One thing I've learned through all of this is that the fight for our children never stops. There are lulls, periods of calm, and there are storms. During the lulls, it's best not to plan too far ahead. Don't worry about what's to come. Just enjoy the calm that moments of peace bring. Celebrate the little wins.

As Jay Shetty writes in his book *Think Like a Monk*, "When you deal with fear and hardship, you realize you are capable of dealing with fear and hardship."[7] This is so true. The only caveat I've noted, from my experience and my work, is that people must CHOOSE to see and acknowledge their ability to deal with these challenges. "Dealing with" looks different from person to person. There's no one right way to deal with something. Throughout life, our response to adversity and struggle also changes. Each struggle adds to our learning and creates opportunities for growth.

Each person has unique influences that guide their decision-making. We all make mistakes, we all encounter crises, and we all work through things in the best way we know how. Once we acknowledge that we can change our perspective and grow through challenge, we can tap into the amazing resilience within. We cannot judge ourselves for how we handled something years ago because of the knowledge we have now.

I can't tell you how many times people in my social circle have said "Wow, Jen, I don't know how you do it" in regards to advocacy, work, and family life. I've heard "I could never do what you do" and "I can't even imagine what you have been through" more times than I care to admit.

These remarks come from a place of kindness but frankly are inaccurate. The reality is, no one knows what they're capable of until they're in a situation. Believe me, I also couldn't have imagined the events that unfolded over the past few years. I didn't know I'd have to teach myself about neurology and brain injury and rehabilitation. I didn't know how chronic the fatigue would be. I didn't know that I'd have to take a crash course in epilepsy during a global pandemic while working from home and attempting to homeschool my kindergarten-aged daughter. I had no idea I'd spend hours trying to learn how to better myself and improve the bond and attachment with my daughter after months of being apart.

Life is unpredictable and full of curveballs. It's not about knowing what pitch is about to be thrown—it's about learning to keep your eye on the ball and knowing that even if you miss, there's something to be learned from the swing.

BEING AUTHENTIC

Recently, a mother of a child living with special needs posted a lovely picture of her family online. In the caption, she mentioned the rare disease her child was living with and made a statement to the effect of "I wouldn't have it any other way."

I felt myself get agitated. *You wouldn't have it any other way? Seriously? If I could make it so that my child lived in a world built to meet the needs of his abilities, I'd do it instantly. In a heartbeat, I would have chosen to not have my family go through this. To not have dealt with hospital stays and being away from one child to care for another. Under no circumstances would I have chosen to have my child lose half his brain to an incurable disease caused by a medical fluke.* Then I immediately felt guilty about my reaction.

One morning after meditating, I sat and reflected on my knee-jerk reaction for a few minutes. Did I really wish this hadn't happened? I'd been focusing on all the things that had come out of the events in our family's life that had made things difficult. But what about the benefits I'd gained from this journey? I'd learned how to cope with my anxiety far better. I'd learned the true meaning of acceptance. I'd learned the power of perspective in a more profound way. I'd stopped feeling pity for people living with disabilities and saw whole, beautiful people instead. I'd started to ask questions and admit when I was wrong (still a work in progress—just ask Paul). I'd learned not to care what other people thought about me or fear their judgment. These are incredible lessons. Would I have learned them without the challenge? I'll never know. I can say that Dominic's medical journey sure put me in the fast lane to these revelations.

Sitting on my couch sipping coffee as the sun rose (a beautiful way to start the day before the kids wake up, although that means starting at 5:15 a.m. in my house—hence the coffee), I continued pondering. And in this moment of silence, I realized how far I'd truly come. I'd learned to find things in this catastrophe that I appreciated. I'd done that. I chose to find the learning. I chose to grow. I chose to be positive. Anyone can do this. But it takes work. It means acknowledging the SUCK that still comes to mind every so often (although less frequently than the first year).

On my road to acceptance there is still grief, sadness, and anguish. These are natural feelings. Acceptance doesn't mean liking an outcome. It means acknowledging that it is what it is. It means taking the positive with the negative. It means that when we experience outcomes we didn't predict nor will, we can choose to see the joy and positivity in life. It's always there if we choose to see it. It's the choosing that can be incredibly difficult. It takes practice.

As I continue this journey of motherhood, I'm continually amazed by how much I learn and am inspired by my children. They are the true teachers of resilience and strength.

THE GOD QUESTION

I'm generally a spiritual person. I was raised in a Catholic household and went to church nearly every Sunday in my childhood. I completed my sacraments and had my children baptized. Before Dominic's stroke, I prayed with the kids nightly and always started and/or ended the day with a moment of gratitude for our home, our family, the food in our bellies, and the life that we had. I always prayed that my children would be able to overcome the challenges they were faced with. I always thanked God for our blessings. Life was good.

After Dominic's stroke, I couldn't bring myself to pray, to talk to God or any higher power. I logically knew that God or the Universe hadn't caused the stroke or this situation, but I was confused, scared, and angry. I needed to direct these feelings somewhere. In a time when I was unable to pray or be in touch with my spirituality and faith, it was comforting to know that those I was closest to were there to do it on my behalf. I told family and friends how grateful I was for their love and support. I believe in the power of positivity and love. I believe energy can be healing. Our family felt the love and strength from our support network, and it helped keep Paul, Dominic, Lorren, and me strong.

During our hospital stay in 2018, I reflected on my spirituality and connection with God. On some level I felt as if we were being punished, even though I knew this sounded silly. There was no known cause for the stroke, and I had nowhere to place blame. So I blamed God and myself. I couldn't even utter the words "Thank God" when I heard good news and would instead say "Thank goodness" or "That's great." I let God hold on to my anger and resentment for a while so that I could focus on being positive and strong for my family.

When I finally got honest with myself (a long time later), I admitted that I felt betrayed. In the ultimate way. Faith was something I'd been taught to trust in. I believed that hardships held lessons. I was brought up with the notion that God has a plan for us all. That we need to seek forgiveness from God when we sin or make mistakes. That He is a healer and a caregiver. That He created the universe.

Family members often told me, "God only gives you what you can handle." *What does this mean, though?* I'd wonder. *Why does someone need to be tested to their limits? If I were a weaker person, would I not have to go through this kind of hardship? If my child weren't as resilient and strong, would he not have had his stroke?* Did this mean God was responsible and we were being challenged to rise to the occasion? That seemed unnecessarily cruel.

The level of anger, resentment, and bitterness a statement like this conjured up in me wasn't healthy. Nothing felt more infuriating or invalidating. The logical part of my brain knew that this was something people said to help others feel better, including themselves. That it was meant to help me feel capable of moving forward and carrying on. It was all very well intentioned. People lean on religion to comfort themselves and others in times of strife. I get that. But very few people were able to sit with me and just say, "This is awful. I'm so sorry you're going through this. I'm here for you." It's hard to do that. I've since worked hard to recognize statements like this for what they are—something to say.

I believed early on that there was a lesson to learn in all of this, but I was infuriated by the thought that my infant had to be the one to endure this experience in order for it to be taught. There was no good enough reason for it in my mind. I had to separate myself from the faith I'd been familiar with for so long. If God was behind what had happened to Dominic and our family, then regardless of the lesson, I didn't think I could ever forgive Him for doing this to an innocent child. This was a good example of my own resistance.

The truth is that this just happened. And I needed to accept that. It was a part of Dominic's journey, and ours too. God didn't DO this to him, or to us. It was a medical fluke. It was horrible and it has changed the course of our lives in many ways. It isn't about the how or why it happened. It's what we do with it that makes the difference. This experience cannot be for nothing. We wouldn't have been put through this just for the sake of going through it—Paul and I made this important acknowledgment to ourselves while Dominic was still in the ICU. We vowed to grow and become stronger. We wanted to use this life-altering experience to help others. Within four days of Dominic's stroke, Paul and I decided to do the fundraiser for the hospital as a form of gratitude. It wasn't much, but it was a start.

When bad things happen, many people lean on their faith for support and strength. I encourage this because the truth is, I never lost my faith. I realized its authenticity for the first time. I'd been following a religious system in which I was raised and that I had a lot of questions about. I stopped turning to the structure of my faith and developed a more personal relationship with it instead. I believe in God, a higher power, the Universe. Call it whatever you like. I trusted the faith of others. I trusted in the power of love and compassion. If God is within everyone around us, it was during this time I truly saw Him for the first time. He was everywhere.

There were days when I felt depleted and exhausted emotionally and physically. I didn't know if I could make it to the next hour. If divine intervention happened, it was in those moments I'd receive messages from family and friends saying that they were thinking of us and sending prayers / positive energy. I felt it. Physically. Emotionally. Mentally. It carried us through the turbulence. It set me back on track when I felt as if my mind were heading toward a void. If that isn't faith in action, I don't know what is.

As confused and upset as I was about what had happened, I couldn't help but be grateful for the positives that still existed. Dominic was alive and had the potential to heal and live a happy, healthy life. As scary, life-changing, and traumatizing as this experience has been, there is still so much to be grateful for. Dominic is a strong, brave, smart, capable boy who will continue to do well. I've always known this. I've felt it in my bones to be the truth.

I believe God helped to guide my family and me through this time. He took my anger and resentment and held on to it for me, no questions asked. He accepted where I was and still provided the support I needed. My faith has changed significantly. It has never been stronger. I no longer go to church every Sunday or say the same memorized prayers daily, but I feel God around me—in my kids, in my husband, in the work I do, in clients I see, in nature. Meditation brings me closer. Prayer is more personal now. It's about trusting my divine ability to channel strength and resilience to get me through the hard times. Because in life, hard times happen, whether we're prepared for them or not.

I've reached a place of acceptance. I don't have the same burning desire to know why this happened. What's important is how I react, how I manage, how I grow. I've seen myself become more understanding, empathetic, accepting, and resilient. I've also seen myself struggle emotionally, mentally, and physically with the stress, worry, fatigue, and burnout that comes with trauma and being a caregiver for a child with special needs. I hate the pain and I love it too because it feeds the growth. I've never known more sadness, grief, and fear than I did in that period of my life. I've gained a deeper sense of love, joy, and compassion from it too. One cannot exist without the other.

Success cannot be truly appreciated without challenge. Growth cannot exist without setbacks. Maybe that's the lesson. And I don't believe I got here on my own. I had help, and I'm thankful for it. For as broken as my heart was and as intense as the hurt felt, the love and joy I feel now is equally as intense.

THE VALUE OF PARADOX

In order to heal, we need to stop trying to push forward. This might seem absurd, as life doesn't stop, whether we're hurting or not. What I mean is that within the hustle and bustle of life, we often fill our time with tasks and to-do lists in hopes of distracting ourselves from the pain we're afraid to touch. We fear that if we open that Pandora's box of emotion and start to feel it all, we may never stop. We may become paralyzed and never move forward. This is a fallacy perpetuated by society.

The "keep calm, carry on" mentality worked in wartime: a time of true limbic response (fight, flight, or freeze—or die). But this isn't a mantra for thriving in daily life. Certain periods of time will be more intense than others. Sometimes, it will make sense to focus on the day to day. This shouldn't be the case for extended periods of time, though. Self-care and healing need to be embedded into the everyday in order for us to thrive and heal and grow in the face of trauma and pain.

Sometimes we need to slow down so that we can run. If you were a runner and injured your knee, you'd either stop training or change up your training to allow for healing before pushing forward and working on attaining your personal bests. The same is true with matters of emotional and mental well-being. We need to stop trying to heal without first feeling the pain. Once we acknowledge that the pain exists, we can start to process it and let it go.

Of course, there are many different experiences and levels of comfort when it comes to doing this. I don't recommend that you start to face traumatic events on your own without support. This is where a therapeutic intervention—a support person to guide you through the process—can be helpful. Once you tune in to what your body needs, it will give you hints regarding when and how to heal.

For as long as I can remember, I've valued my ability to see the glass as half full. "Could be worse" is something I used to say a lot. I had no understanding of how I was invalidating my experiences. I was also elevating myself above others who "had it worse" in my mind. At that time, this was a coping tool. Focusing on what could be worse was a way for me to look at what I was grateful for, or what brought joy to my life. I didn't realize that I could do that while also acknowledging pain, sadness, and anger. I still believe that there are different levels of challenge and suffering, but my understanding of this has changed dramatically.

SPEAKING DIFFERENT LANGUAGES

In the summer of 2021, our family dealt with the loss of loved ones—patriarchs within my extended family and Paul's. During the funeral events, we saw family that we hadn't seen since well before the pandemic. Before the seizure explosion. They'd seen snippets of our life on social media or heard about what was happening from mutual family members, but they didn't know what we'd actually been through.

Many of them asked how the kids were doing and then asked specifically about Dominic's healing. Hemispherectomies aren't common, but there's ample information available through trusted sources online. I'd forget that others hadn't done the hours and hours of research we had. I used to get frustrated with the lack of understanding. I used to get upset when people made assumptions. That people didn't see how some of their comments could be hurtful.

One time, we were taking a photo of the kids and a family member suggested I take it again and reposition Dominic's arm to hide his floppy left wrist because it didn't look "right." That hit like a sucker punch to the gut. I bluntly replied, "I will not take another picture. This is what his wrist looks like sometimes. People who don't like it don't have to look at the picture." And then I walked away. It wasn't up to me to protect others' fragility. I no longer needed to placate. Feeling the fury rise in my chest, I took some space. I was upset about the hurt this could have caused had Dominic heard it, and the lack of forward thinking and body positivity that the world desperately needs.

Upon reflection (and after settling my emotions through deep breathing and taking space), I realized something. When people speak this way, it has nothing to do with the recipient of the message. It has everything to do with the person delivering the message. People use their own languages to show support, curiosity, care, and concern. They might know only one language. In this case, that family member was expressing love and concern for my child, worried that people might have a negative reaction. Did this person need to be corrected? Absolutely. Did I need to hold on to anguish and resentment? No.

For a while, I was concerned that I might never feel connected to some people again. Spending so much time just the four of us and going through what we went through without much opportunity for family support had created a bit of a silo. Then I remembered that no matter what people understood, it was likely that their intentions were good. If I was bothered, that was on me, not them. It was a reminder that I had more healing to do. I likely have healing to do for the rest of my life. The difference now is that I'm no longer comparing my journey to anyone else's. They're all different.

I started to translate messages as I received them, reminding myself that people are generally well intentioned and those who aren't have no place in our lives. Setting boundaries became a bit easier.

Paul and I are also processing this journey in incredibly different ways and at different speeds. It's not about always being on the same page. It's about being able to communicate what's on our respective pages and respecting each other's processes. Communicating concerns, compassion, and understanding. Remembering that we've chosen to be on the same team, and that this doesn't mean playing the same position or having the same strengths. It means valuing our differences and doing our best to support and coach each other.

FIFTEEN

The Beginning

One year after Dominic's hemispherectomy, I look back at all that has taken place. At how far we've come, how much I've learned. It seems as if a lifetime has been lived in the past five years. I was broken down into pieces and have begun putting them back together. The puzzle of who I am and how I live is different now. There are new pieces finding their place. There are pieces of me that will always wonder why this happened, that will never understand. That's okay. I accept that. I don't always need to have an answer. In letting go of that need, I've allowed myself to learn so much more. I've gained perspective. I've learned so much about neuroplasticity and the ability to regain lost functions after a brain injury, and I've used these concepts to inform how I treat my mental health and my clients'.

Dominic has started kindergarten and Lorren is in grade two. Their first day of school was huge, filled with hugs and smiles and tears from Paul and me. Another group of adults is responsible for providing care to our son for part of the day, and accepting this felt big. It has taken many hours of planning, advocacy, letdowns, frustrations, hope, and trust to get here. Seeing our son adjust to mainstream school has been incredible. He requires additional support and accommodations for his learning, but we're just starting to see what he's capable of. This has provided Paul and me with optimism and inspiration around what we, too, are capable of.

To this day, I repeat this mantra with the kids before bed: "I am strong, I am smart, I am brave, I am kind, I am loved, I am enough. I can work hard. I can do hard things. I love myself just the way I am."

I've learned that I need to feel the emotions within and around me in order to heal and move forward. Sometimes that means taking a pause, being easier on myself, and showing some compassion and forgiveness to myself and others. This allows me to see the rainbow after the storm, not just the puddles.

I don't know what the future holds. I have goals and dreams, and I have a deep appreciation for the fact that no matter what the storm brings, we can pick up the pieces of debris and rebuild. Rebuild our family and ourselves. Each time we do this, our whole is stronger and more beautiful than before. I trust in the process. I also forgive myself whenever I get caught up in the worry. And then I focus on the wonder. Instead of needing to curate the path to get there, I'm learning to let go and enjoy the journey. We've got the rest of our lives to figure it out. And it looks pretty good from here.

A Final Note

Remember, on the journey of life you may fall flat on your face. When this happens, though, your head is still in front of where your feet were—and that's progress. It might hurt like hell. It might not be pretty. But it's progress. It's only when we fall that we learn how to get back up and keep on going. You're always growing. The hardest experiences are the best opportunities for learning.

Keep growing. You've got this.
With love,
Jen

Key Takeaways

WHEN DEALING WITH A CRISIS:

- Contact your closest support people but don't spend too much time providing details. Keep it brief and basic.
- Minimize the number of calls you make. Set up a point-of-contact person; to avoid retraumatization, have them disseminate information so that you aren't repeating it multiple times.
- Don't tell people it will be okay.
- Identify your shock and give it permission to exist.
- Arrange transportation if needed. Do NOT drive if you're in shock.
- Protect your energy.
- Answer calls ONLY when you have the energy and time to do so. If you don't get back to people right away, it's okay. Let them know it'll be a while (if you can). If they have a problem with it, that speaks volumes about them and has nothing to do with you.

- Get a notebook and TAKE NOTES. Whip it out when doctors do their rounds, when meetings are held, when you meet new people, and when a question pops into your head and you fear you might forget it.
- Gather personal effects to carry you through for longer than one day (delegate this to someone else on your behalf, if possible).
- Confirm childcare for other kids as required.
- Acknowledge how you're feeling. Even if you aren't feeling. Acknowledge the numb.
- Take deep, diaphragmatic breaths. If you find yourself feeling out of control and needing something to do to stay occupied and feel useful, consider the following:

LET. IT. GO.

- Relinquish control. It was never yours anyway.
- Let others in. Let them help. Give up the practical items on the to-do list where possible. Take anything you can off your plate and DO NOT give it another thought. If people are willing to help, let them.
- ASK for help. If you need someone to listen, tell them that. Tell people what you need. People want to help. Your job is to let them. It not only helps you, but it also gives others purpose and fulfillment—they get to help you in a time of strife. Asking will get easier. Looking back, I see how big the village was that held our family together during this period, and I'm so full of love for all these people.

WHEN BECOMING AN ADVOCATE:

- Ask questions. Get clarity.
- Voice your concerns. Don't be afraid to stand up for what you're fighting for.
- Be the voice that someone needs but doesn't have right now.
- Remember that no one will fault you for doing what's best for your loved one. If they do, it says a lot more about them than you.

WHEN IN A RELATIONSHIP DURING A CRISIS:

- Be prepared to ACCEPT each other's differences. And to respect them.
- Don't assume that your partner knows what's going on in your head. Each person is different. We all process things differently, especially trauma.
- Remember that there is no right way to manage. Try your best to show up for your partner, and always show up for yourself.
- Own the times when you cannot be there for them.
- See your differences as complementary rather than adversarial.
- Know that the hard times provide the best opportunity for growth and positive change. Take them in stride.
- Communicate with your partner. Always.
- Please, please remember to laugh. Laugh whenever you can.

WHEN HEALING:

- Have hope. This is key. In the darkest of times, we don't need much light to see. We just have to look with intention.
- Take care of yourself, always. The phrase "fill your cup so you can help others" implies pouring from your own. Try filling your cup and using the OVERFLOW to help others. Protect your peace.
- Remind yourself that you've made it through 100 percent of the worst days of your life up to now.
- Find out what parts of you no longer fit and what parts of you have changed and begin rewriting your narrative. You are the author of your own life.
- Remember that a best effort is a subjective measure. Some days the best is amazing. Other days the best is simply surviving.
- Celebrate the smallest wins.
- Notice the learning and growing that happens over time.
- Know that being strong means accessing the spectrum of emotions and opening up. Being strong means accepting the negative emotions and feeling them. Owning them. Knowing that no matter how terrible and scary it feels, you can get through this, and it will get better.
- Give yourself grace, forgiveness, love, and understanding.
- Allow space for crying and grief.
- OPEN UP about how you're feeling. Find a network of people who've gone through a similar experience.
- Treat yourself as if you are your best friend. Speak to yourself differently. Try being gentle. Try acceptance.

Acknowledgments

I'd like to take a moment to thank the MANY people in our village who have supported my family and me along this journey. Without them, this book wouldn't have happened, and I might not be the person I am today. I could write love letters to everyone, but that would be another book entirely.

To our parents: None of what we achieve would be possible without your support. From babysitting to food, hand-me-downs, and home-improvement projects, you guys have been there for everything. We're eternally grateful, and we know that how we parent is a direct outcome of how we were raised.

To our siblings: Thank you for showing up when we've needed you. During the light and darkness. For caring for our children as if they were your own. We love you and are so grateful.

To extended family: If you know us, you know our family is huge. Thank you to our cousins, aunts, and uncles for supporting our family with positive thoughts, prayers, guidance, generosity, and love. It truly carried us through some of the darkest times. Our village is so strong, and we know this isn't the case for many people. We love you and appreciate you.

To our closest friends (you know who you are): Thank you for being the best friends Paul and I could ask for. You and your families have offered us support and generosity for which we'll forever be grateful.

To all the medical moms and dads we've met along the way: Thank you for your authenticity. For showing me your grit, determination, vulnerabilities, and character. You have inspired me on my own journey. You inspire me in how you love your children and navigate the choppy waters of the healthcare and education systems with grace, honesty, determination, and humor. In some cases, I think our paths were destined to cross, and although the circumstances were ones we'd never wish on our worst enemy, I'm grateful that they brought these friendships into my life as a result.

To the staff at SickKids and Holland Bloorview Kids Rehabilitation Hospital: No words will ever describe our feeling of gratitude for the care you provided our child and us. Your patience and your passion for your work show. We're so grateful to be a car ride away from these world-class establishments made renowned because of the people within them. Thank you for saving my son's life and helping him learn to live again. You saved mine too.

End Notes

1. Canadian Stroke Best Practices, "Pediatric Stroke," Heart and Stroke Foundation, accessed November 2, 2022, https://www.strokebestpractices.ca/recommendations/pediatric-stroke.

2. Heart and Stroke Foundation, *Canadian Stroke Best Practice Recommendations*, 5th Edition, 2016, https://heartstrokeprod.azureedge.net/-/media/1-stroke-best-practices/csbpr_summary-of-pediatric-recommendations_5th-edition_final_2016may4.ashx?rev=40a52b08b4d749eca6d66faa978e6acd.

3. SickKids staff, "Childhood stroke: Arterial ischemic stroke (AIS)," The Hospital for Sick Children, accessed November 2, 2022, https://www.aboutkidshealth.ca/Article?contentid=854&language=English.

4. Brené Brown, *Rising Strong: How the Ability to Reset Transforms the Way We Live, Love, Parent, and Lead* (Random House, 2015).

5. Gabor Maté, *When the Body Says No: The Cost of Hidden Stress* (Vintage Canada, 2004).

6. (2019, August). Second Opinions (Episode 2). J. Chinn, S. Chinn, P.G. Morgan, J. Silverstein, G. Bausch, E. Bush, S. Rudin, M. Moul, A. Braverman (Executive Producers), *Diagnosis*. Lightbox. Scott Rudin Productions.

7. Jay Shetty, *Think Like a Monk: Train Your Mind for Peace and Purpose Every Day* (Simon & Schuster, 2020).

YGTMedia Co. is a blended boutique publishing house for mission-driven humans. We help seasoned and emerging authors "birth their brain babies" through a supportive and collaborative approach. Specializing in narrative nonfiction and adult and children's empowerment books, we believe that words can change the world, and we intend to do so one book at a time.

🌐 ygtmedia.co/publishing

📷 @ygtmedia.co

f @ygtmedia.co

Made in the USA
Las Vegas, NV
22 March 2023

69557700R00144